# Introductory Guide to
# IT CONCEPTS

# Introductory Guide to
# IT CONCEPTS

CJ Rhoads

## Supplemental book to:

*Microsoft Office in Business*
Joseph Manzo, CJ Rhoads, published by Prentice Hall
A Pearson Education Company

*The Entrepreneur's Guide to Managing Information Technology*
CJ Rhoads, published by Praeger Group/Greenwood Publishing

**Custom Publishing**

New York   Boston   San Francisco
London   Toronto   Sydney   Tokyo   Singapore   Madrid
Mexico City   Munich   Paris   Cape Town   Hong Kong   Montreal

Printed in the United States of America

10  9  8  7  6  5  4  3  2  1

2008820020

MP/MJ

**Pearson
Custom Publishing**
is a division of

www.pearsonhighered.com

ISBN 10: 0-555-05108-0
ISBN 13: 978-0-555-05108-5

# *Dedication*

I dedicate this book to Mark Dinger, who pioneered in developing the information systems courses in the College of Business at Kutztown University. In the next year, Mark plans to hang up his keyboard teaching the Business 171 course to all the incoming freshman at Kutztown University. Unfortunately, the students will be the poorer for it, for he was a marvelous teacher. Mark approached the very difficult field of Information Technology with openness and gusto, and he has been a true mentor for me as I learned how to adjust to the Kutztown academic culture.

I also dedicate this book to my students, who find me "a little crazy" (as one student commented) " but great once you get used to her". I continue to find wonder and grace among the wide-eyed youth who fill the seats of my computer lab each semester. When they work hard and *get it*, I don't know who is more thrilled - them or me. If they only knew how hard it was for me to *get it* thirty years ago when I started in this field - the hours, days, and weeks I spent in frustration trying to get the %^&*#$@ computer to do what it was supposed to do - they would know that I understand their frustration, but recognize it as a necessary obstacle which must be overcome.

Finally, I must dedicate this book to my wonderful loving husband, Bob. He is my life and my world, and I am so lucky to have found my soul mate and true love so early in my life. To have spent the past 28 years with a man of his incredible talents would have been a treat to anyone, but to have loved him, and been loved by him, all that time is a pleasure of epic proportion.

# Table of Contents

# Illustrations

## Figures

## *Tables*

# Acknowledgements

As those who have their names on the cover of a book know, no book is written solely by the author. A good book cannot exist without an entire team of people, and it is only by convention and convenience (not to mention space) that not all of those names appear on the cover. They are no less responsible for its birth than I.

Of major importance is T. Max Devlin, a brilliant networking educator who taught me everything I know about networks, and not just because he is my brother. Much of the material in this book came from *Enterprise Network Management,* published by Hi-TECH Educational Services, authored by Max and edited by yours truly. Although Max has sworn off the computer industry, his educational know-how lives on in the people he has taught.

I would also like to thank the faculty and staff of the College of Business (in alphabetical order): Okan Akcay, Dan Benson, Pat Blatt, Henry Check, Donna DeLong, Arifeen Daneshyar, Mark Dinger, Ken Ehrensal, Tom Grant, Keshav Gupta, David Haas, John Hamrick, Ray Heimbach, Roger Hibbs, Eileen Hogan, Fidel Ikem, Jonathan Kramer, John Kruglinski, James "Doc" Ogden, Patricia Patrick, Elisabeth Rogol, Paul Sable, Norman Sigmond, David Wagaman, and John Walker. Their encouragement and support enabled me to get this book done.  . Additionally, I thank the employees of my business: Stella Deeble, George Deeble who all had to put up with my split focus while I was writing.

Of course none of this would be possible without my many mentors over the years (in alphabetical order): Fred Beste, Mike Bolton, David Bosler, Jack Bradt, Tom Casey, Betsy Chapman, Martin Cheatle, Jim Collins, Vanessa DiMauro, Jonathan Dreazen, Francois Dumas, Marsha Egan, Dale Falcinelli, John Lucht, John MacNamara, Nancy Magee, Ray Melcher, Pete Musser, Maggie Newman, Josephine Painter, Joe Puglisi, Leo Robb, Robert Rubin, Lee Scheele, Steve Sperling, Alan Weiss, and Kevin Wren. Though the amount of time I spent with each varied, each one has given me a gift that has turned out to be of extreme value in my never-ending quest to improve myself.

# Introduction

*Introductory Guide to Information Technology (IT) Concepts* is a book written to address the minimal needs for business students and business owners to understand the basics of technology. It is not a history of computers, though there are interesting historical tidbits distributed throughout. It is not an exhaustive or academic explanation of every term or concept in IT, but rather a focused introduction on the terms and concepts that will help business people to understand the technology upon which businesses rely. This book focuses specifically on the common misunderstandings and key concepts that are necessary for business people trying to make decisions regarding information technology.

In addition to being a supplemental textbook in an introductory business information technology course, it is also a supplement to *Entrepreneur's Guide to Managing Information Technology* published by Praeger in April of 2008. While that book focuses on high-level practical advice for business leaders, this book focuses on explaining the underlying information technology concepts.

## Why You Should Read This Book

In today's computer driven environment, everyone in business from students to senior leaders needs to know and understand the basics of information technology. There is a raft of books on various hardware and software applications. There are hundreds of generic "Introduction to Computers" books. But in each one, there is usually one of two missing elements; context or simplicity.

Textbooks and popular books on information technology alike either try to explain in too much detail (and therefore lose the interest of the reader), or simplify the concepts so much that the necessary key knowledge gets lost. Students and business people alike need a short but effective introduction to information technology terminology and concepts; both computer-related and network-related.

This book will introduce basic concepts in context, making them easier to understand and apply. *Introductory Guide to Information Technology Concepts* will contain enough information to lay a strong foundation for further work and experience of the reader or student. It will include practical advice as well as interesting stories, and information about real companies providing hardware and software.

## Learning a New Language

Learning about IT necessitates learning a whole new language - harder than learning Spanish or French because often you can't point to something in order to name it. While it may be frustrating to encounter so many words, phrases, and acronyms initially, it is important to remember that they are not there simply to confuse people. Every time a technology person designed something new, that person had to name the innovation. Every time a vendor wanted to market a new product or service, they had to name the product or service. As a result, there are thousands of new words, phrases, and acronyms that either didn't exist in the general language in previous decades, or meant something completely different.

# Chapter 1: Revolutions

Many people believe that the introduction of the personal computer in the eighties "changed everything" much like the introduction of the telephone "changed everything" and the introduction of the combustion engine "changed everything".

However - in 1992, those with computers were still in the minority even though personal computers had been around for over ten years. Computers were still mostly at work (not in the home). Computers at that time did very specific tasks and ran very specific programs. Except for a few hobbyists who played games and enjoyed learning to program, a computer was not a commonly seen item. In 1992, the first really stable computer hardware/software that could be used by normal everyday people (instead of just the technically adept) had just come out.[1]

Fast forward another ten years, however, and it is a different world. More homes in the United States have computers than don't have computers. Email is as essential to business as a telephone. Many businesses are pure "web based" and don't even have a physical building. Every major business has a web page - often thousands of web pages - enabling customers to do research on products and services. From purchasing to delivering to paying, many businesses conduct the entire process completely over the Internet.

## Why You Need to Understand Revolutions

It is important to understand the technological events that impact the IT world because they explain some of the seemingly strange situations. For example, it would be a mistake (a common mistake, but a mistake just the same) to think that the sudden growth of personal computers came about solely because of the Internet[2]. To better understand today's technology, it makes sense to look at the "subrevolutions" impacting the current state of affairs.

---

[1] Some consider the Intel x486 chip with Microsoft Windows 3.1 operating system the "first stable useful personal computer". Others may argue that the Macintosh was better, but the proprietary nature of Apple technology, (as compared to the "open hardware standards" architecture of the personal computers with the x486 chip), meant that the Macintosh would be considered a "niche" machine for education and art/publishing, whereas the PC was a general purpose business machine that could be used in thousands of situations.

[2] The Internet is a world wide network of connected computers. The World Wide Web is the system of linking that works over the network of connected computers. Think of the Internet as the roadway system, and the World Wide Web as the cars and trucks that run on the roads. More details on this will be explained in a later chapter.

# Six Sub-Revolutions

Basically, there were six subrevolutions after the introduction of the personal computer in the 80s:

➢ Breaking the 640K Barrier,

➢ Standardizing the Internet and World Wide Web,

➢ Dot Com Fever,

➢ Fiber Glut,

➢ Switch To Digital, and

➢ First Mile Crisis.

## *Breaking the 640K Barrier*

One of those little technical details that few outside of the technical worlds of hardware and software understand is the impact, in the early days of computers, of the huge expense of memory and hard drive space. Mainframe programmers would specialize in getting programs to run in the typical **2 k bytes**[3] of memory available in the seventies and early eighties on the huge mainframes. Whole industries were developed out of the need to fit more programming in less and less space. Every byte saved made the computers cost less.

The focus on saving memory and storage set the stage for a technical limitation called *The 640k Barrier*. Early PCs had a built-in limitation of 640 kilobytes of active memory that could be used. When this limitation was established, a top-of-the-line million-dollar mainframe computer had **64 k bytes** of memory. It was reasonable to make the technical limit 10 times that amount for a microcomputer . it was not thought that anyone would need that much memory[4]. Similarly, the typical hard drive was 10 Megabytes, so the limit of hard drive space that could be addressed was established as 2,000,000 Megabytes (or 2 Gigabytes), again much more than anyone thought would be needed by a personal computer. Filling up 20 megabytes of hard drive space was unthinkable. A computer with 1 gigabyte of hard drive space cost over $5000. Most mainframe computers still stored data on large magnetic tapes because hard drive space was simply too expensive. Personal computers used 5 1/4 inch floppy disks that stored less than 1 meg.

The problem was that, while 640k memory was more than enough in a text-based computer world, it wasn't even a blip in the memory needs of a graphic world. When operating systems like the Macintosh and Windows started adding little pictures and menus that could be clicked on with a mouse, the existing memory and hard drive space requirements were simply not enough. The key concept to remember is that the difference between the mem-

---

[3] A typical personal computer these days has 2,000,000 k bytes of memory (2 gigabytes). More details on memory and hard drives can be found in a later chapter.

[4] You may hear reference to a quote by Bill Gates stating "Who in their right mind would ever need more than 640k of RAM!?". Bill Gates, however, denies that he ever said that.

ory/storage needs of text and the memory/storage needs of graphics is **huge**. (There's another huge leap from graphics to video as well, but that will be discussed in a later chapter.)

For years the personal computer industry hobbled along, and people who wanted to use Windows or any other graphical user interface had to purchase memory managers and learn the difference between "real" memory and "virtual" memory. Since every peripheral used up memory, there was a severe limitation on how many devices could be attached to computers, and attaching a new one could guarantee days of trial and error in changing "interrupts" and remapping the existing memory to accommodate the new devices.

Then came Windows 95, 98, and 98SE, and ME[5]. The Windows operating systems of this era were basically the same version going from buggy to stable to unstable (a typical product life cycle for operating systems). Windows 95 introduced two phenomenal features that made it much more user friendly than any other operating system (with the exception of the Macintosh which was always friendly but too expensive and without the business support of the PC world.) *Virtual Memory Management* was a feature whereby the operating system itself managed the memory so that the 640k barrier, in the eyes of the end user, disappeared. (It was actually still there, but because part of the hard drive could be used as if it were memory, the technical barrier disappeared from the point of view of the software, so many more programs could be run at the same time.) The other feature was *Plug and Play* device installation. When a new device was attached to a computer, Windows 95 would try to identify it and install the proper drivers so that the new device would work[6]

Why would these two seemingly tiny technical details make such a difference? Because it made it possible for someone, without any technical training at all, to buy, install, and use a personal computer. Huge numbers of people went ahead and did just that. This PC proliferation established a base of people who were in a position for the next level; the Internet and the World Wide Web.

### *Standardizing the Internet and World Wide Web*

With a large installed base of personal computers, the stage was set for people to be able to communicate with each other using these computers. Although local area networks had been around for years (which enabled computers in the same building to communicate) and wide area networks had been around even longer (which enabled a single computer to communicate with another single computer far away), in 1992 connecting with another computer was still, by and large, something that only technical people did. In the world of networking there were hundreds of different protocols. Each protocol had its own way of doing things, its own rules for communication between computers. Each protocol needed its

---

[5] These are operating systems for personal computers. An operating system provides the instructions for the system; how the keyboard works, how the hard drive works, how the monitor works, etc. More details in later chapters.

[6] A *driver* is a tiny file that contains the instructions for the device so that the operating system knows how to access that particular device like printers and cameras and monitors, etc. Many drivers come with the operating system, but some need to be provided by the device manufacturer.

own type of device and connection, and few of them talked to each other.  Again - whole industries arose around getting different networks to interconnect.   There were special devices (called bridges and switches) to convert one type of network into another type of network.  **But in 1992 the network of one company almost never communicated with the network of another company.**

Then in the early nineties, the US government handed over management of the Internet into the hands of private commercial ventures.  At the same time, Timothy Berners-Lee and Robert Cailliau developed an easy-to-use interface (a system of hyperlinks) that worked with the Internet.  The system of hyperlinking is called the World Wide Web.  Because of the Internet and the World Wide Web, suddenly[7], someone with no technical training at all could connect to any other computer on the Internet network, and could retrieve information from any of those computers.  All they had to know how to do was click a mouse.

## *Dot Com Fever*

In the latter part of the nineties, the business world took notice of new technologies popping up. One of the first companies to take advantage of the personal computers on people's desks and the World Wide Web was **eBay**, which incorporated in 1995.  eBay put buyers in touch with sellers (but did not sell or buy anything themselves).  This marked the launch of a period of time that many refer to as the **Internet Boom** or **Technology Bubble** which lasted until February of 2001.  During this time, many people saw the power of the Internet and information technology in a new light. Many invested heavily in any technology company that sounded good.  After all - the business they invested in might be the next Microsoft!  Venture capital was easy to get, and did not require years of profits as had been required in the past.  Thousands of companies, financed with venture capital, started on the road to make millions in the revolutionary new world where every home had a computer and was connected to the Internet and every business network could easily connect to every other business network.

Companies that had an actual product and profitable years were being pushed out for companies with a great idea and no hope of profitability in the near future.  It was called (with a straight face) the "new economy" where sizzle was more important than steak.  But there were some people urging caution.  In a now-famous 1998 speech, Federal Reserve Chairman Alan Greenspan warned the financial world of impending collapse by calling the over-investing in information technology "irrational exuberance".

As can be expected, the boom did not last forever.  Indeed, the dot-com frenzy was followed by a deep crash.  Instead of wild speculation and investors being easy to find, people were losing money in the millions and venture capital had dried up completely.  Companies went out of business by the thousands as the "new economy" proved to be more shadow than substance.  The real-life influence of the World Trade Center being destroyed on September

---

[7]Well, it felt like suddenly, but actually it took many years.  The Internet started functioning in 1982, and the World Wide Web was invented in 1990.  More details on both will be found in later chapters.

11, 2001 did not help the economy, and the entire business world, especially information technology industries, went into a depression that lasted years.

Nonetheless, one of the industries that received the most funding during the boom times was fiber optics. Newly formed fiber optics companies bought up rights-of-way and laid fiber optic cable in preparation for the coming need for connections between cities. This investment led to the next phase, the Fiber Glut.

## Fiber Glut

The dot com era provided the capital and the kick in the pants necessary to solve many of the technical problems that had previously prevented easy data communications. One of the outcomes of the dot com crash, however, was the sudden glut on the market of fiber optic services. All those newly formed companies to take advantage of the coming need for high quality connectivity were sold for pennies on the dollar, lowering the cost for connecting to the Internet. This provided real competition to the un-competitive leased data line[8] business that previously only the local phone company could provide. In response, the phone companies also increased their fiber capacity to prevent being left behind. The quality and capacity of the highways between cities improved drastically during the years of the technology bubble.

This fiber glut also contributed to the increasing globalization we all keep hearing about. Because of cheap fiber crossing the oceans, it became feasible to outsource tasks and functions like programming, transcriptions, and customer service to India, China, Russia, and dozens of other countries[9].

There was still a problem, however. The high expense of getting from the fiber highways to the individual homes and businesses where people could use the broadband capacity remained. Basically there were superhighways going from country to country and city to city, but there were few entry and exit ramps. This was known in technology circles as the Last Mile crisis.

---

[8] Before the Internet, if a business wanted to connect one computer to another computer, it had to lease a direct phone line between the two computers. This was known as a leased data line, and was sold, usually, as a T-1 line or a Frame Relay. More details will be explained in a later chapter.

[9] An excellent description by a non-technologist of the impact of globalization on business can be found in Thomas L. Friedman's *The World Is Flat* published by Farrar, Straus, and Giroux in 2005

## First Mile Crisis

The phrase *the Last Mile crisis* refers to the inconvenience and lack of ease in getting broad bandwidth[10] to the "last mile" between the phone companies and the individual homes and businesses. In 2002, the Last Mile crisis was estimated to cost **365 billion dollars** to solve in the US alone – and that the problem was much worse in other countries.

Calling the problem the "last mile" illustrates how technologists tend to put the technology first instead of the customer. It's only the LAST mile if you think of the technology as the center. It's the FIRST mile if you think of the customer as the center. Early on there was a movement to change the terminology from the "Last Mile" crisis to the "First Mile" crisis to indicate the switch in focus from the technology to the customer.

Whether it is called the last mile or the first mile, there are three paths to a solution, and in 2002 no one knew which path would be the one which would work the best:
1. technology that provides broadband over existing wiring to the home
2. laying fiber cable to the homes and businesses, or
3. providing wireless broadband access

At the time, companies and individuals were still paying $300 - 1000 a month for a point to point leased line connections to the Internet to get broadband speeds (or suffering with slow dialup connections over telephone lines). In the United States, of the three paths, the first one has become the most common. Digital Subscriber Lines (DSL) and Cable Modems are the broadband option of choice for most people in order to connect to the Internet for the first mile. Soon, however, the second choice may overtake the first option as FIber Optic Service [FiOS]) becomes more available. At the present time, FiOS is only available in big city areas.

However, it must be noted that for thirty percent of the population in the United States, the third option (wireless broadband) is the only option because many people don't live or work near enough to the switching equipment to get either broadband or fiber. In other countries (especially Asia and Europe), wireless broadband is the more common solution. However; wireless broadband is still expensive and somewhat unreliable compared to the other two solutions. So the first mile crisis is still a problem - though going away quickly.

## Switch To Digital

As the First Mile Crisis is being solved, the next revolution is in full growth mode; the switch to digital everything. Instead of analog cameras where the negatives must be developed, we use digital cameras and store the pictures on memory sticks or hard drives. Instead of using analog phones, people are purchasing Voice Over Internet Protocol (VOIP) phones because calling next door and calling Japan costs the same over the Internet. Even cell phones are all-digital these days (though a different kind of digital than VOIP).

---

[10] Bandwidth is the term we use to describe the speed and or size of a network connection. Broadband refers to having a faster and/or bigger connection. More technical details can be found in the later chapters.

Instead of paper checks, a copy of your check has been digitized and can be viewed on-line. Films and movies are released on Digital Video Disc (DVD) instead of on reels or videotape. Research is hardly ever printed in paper journals anymore; digital access makes it ever-so-much-easier to learn what other experts are doing and add onto their findings rather than reinventing the wheel.

The advantages to digital data are many.
1. Digital storage takes up much less room than paper.
2. Digital connections are cheaper than analog connections.
3. Digital data can be easily searched and indexed.
4. Digital data can be copied and shared much more easily and cheaper than paper.
5. Digital data is easier to manipulate and edit than non-digital data.
6. Digital data can be viewed and/or downloaded on-line.

The impact of this switch to digital for businesses cannot be over-emphasized. Many business processes describe the movement of forms (often in multi-part copies of white, pink, green, and goldenrod where each department gets their copy and passes the rest on to another department). If the form is digitized instead, the form doesn't physically have to move from place to place. If placed on the internet, the form can be accessed by anyone in the company in any office anywhere - all at the same time. If we separate the data itself from the form, we can digitize the information without creating a graphic view of the form; enabling a much more flexible process.

For example, imagine a business process for requesting and approving funds for a capital project within a business. In the non-digital manual process, the physical form is sent through postal mail to four different offices, in sequence, to get the proper authorizing signatures (often being Fed Ex'd from Wilmington to Texas to Boston and back to Wilmington). The average time for the request to be approved might be 40 days (not very fast).

In the digital scenario, the form would become a series of fill-in-blanks on a web page. Instead of postal mail (known as *snail mail* in technology circles) or Fed Ex, the information would be emailed to all four senior leaders who need to authorize the expense. They could simply reply with "approved" or "rejected". The average time for approval might get shortened from 41 days to 2 days. Imagine the cost savings in personnel and postage (especially since the speed of business commonly compelled people to FedEx the forms). Imagine the change in the speed of new projects getting started, new client acquisition, new sources of revenues to start. To remain competitive, businesses must understand the switch to digital and take advantage of it.

## The Next Revolution

The next revolution will be around video technologies. Once the infrastructure is in place, videoconferencing will be as ubiquitous as telephones are today. It must be noted, however, that despite current trends which point out this fact, ubiquitous video is still decades away.

For one thing, videoconferencing is still pretty expensive. In addition to the high cost of the equipment itself, the price of the connection between any two videoconferencing sites is pretty steep. Additionally, most videoconferencing is still "point to point". In other words, the connection has to be a special connection made just for videoconferencing from one place to another.

Some people think that because they can use free services (such as Skype) to videoconference with friends and family halfway around the world, that day is already here. True, if the stars align just right, webcams are possible. But they are not easy or practical (yet). Our brains automatically reel against video that is less than television quality. Jerky movements, sudden freezing, words that don't match the mouths or faces that occasionally pixelate into unrecognizability; all of these are side effects of poor quality typical of internet-based videoconferencing. Such video is worse than no picture at all.

Despite its present-day drawbacks, videoconferencing will continue to improve until it is feasible, easy, and cheap. Wall-sized video screens (called *telepresence*) will have a major impact on businesses and education everywhere. Why worry about getting a corner office with a window when you can display beautiful live views of the Rocky Mountains on your entire wall? Why worry about traveling when you can see your friends and neighbors sitting at your table as clearly as you see them now? Add a wii interface[11] and you can golf and fish with your buddies without ever leaving the room. Why even travel to a building in a city to work when the entire team can meet more efficiently virtually from home? What reason would there be for working in cities and polluting our air with cars once people can connect, in full size, in person, without traveling?

Back in the sixties, Isaac Asimov wrote a science fiction story about a universe where people never met face to face because they could conduct all their business and do all their socializing through room-sized videoconferencing. While life may not become that extreme, once the quality and the infrastructure are there, video telepresence will be everywhere. And it will change the world, again.

---

[11] Wii is a hands-on video game technology that enables you to play physical games like golf and tennis virtually.

# Obeying the Law

Within the world of business, there are several "laws" that are familiar to everyone. Murphy's law (proposed by Capt. Edward A. Murphy in 1949) is that if anything can go wrong, it will. The Peter Principle (proposed by Dr. Lawrence Peter and Raymond Hull in 1968) is that in a hierarchy every employee tends to rise to his level of incompetence. Recognition of the truth in these laws (actually more like rules of thumb) can help avoid problems in the future.

Within the world of technology, there are various "laws" that have been proposed and have proven themselves useful. These laws can help people understand just what and why certain technology changes occur (and why other aspects of technology never seem to progress). Knowing the laws can help business people make better technology decisions. We will explain five laws, all named after the person who proposed them[12]:

- ♦ Moore's Law
- ♦ Metcalf's Law
- ♦ Gilder's Law
- ♦ Loewy's Law
- ♦ Jakob's Law

Gordon Moore (Intel co-founder) proposed in 1965 what is now known as Moore's law; that *the number of transistors that can be placed on an integrated circuit* (i.e. - the power of a computer chip) *will increase exponentially, approximately doubling every two years.* This has resulted in a drop in price and an increase in power for computers every eighteen months or so.

In the 1980s, Bob Metcalfe (founder of 3COM and inventor of Ethernet) proposed what is now known as Metcalf's law: *the value of a network grows as a square of the number of nodes* (i.e. computers) *on the network.* Many people have attributed this underlying truth as a reason for the explosive growth of the Internet.

In 2000, George Gilder, an author and technology pundit, expanded and connected the first two laws by proposing that *bandwidth grows at least three times faster than computing power*. Considering the issue of the Fiber Glut and the increased demand for faster connections, this law has proven pretty useful. (Gilder also predicted that broadcast television would become obsolete because of "telecomputers" connected to broadband fiber cable. [13])

Jakob's Law (named after Jakob Nielsen, the father of web interface design) noted that users spend most of their time on **other** *sites*. Thus, anything that is a convention and used on the majority of other sites will be burned into the users' brains and web developers can only deviate from it on pain of major usability problems.

---

[12] More laws can be found on http://sysprog.net/quotlaws.html, a site sponsored by Syspro.net, a firm in Atlanta, Georgia that caters to IBM system 360 programmers.

[13] Gilder, George. (1985) *Life After Television* by W. W. Norton & Company, New York.

Raymond Loewy, the father of modern industrial design, coined the phrase MAYA - Most Advanced Yet most Acceptable - to describe public acceptance of technology. It served as a guiding law for Loewy and those in his employ; reminding them not to push a design, however excellent, beyond the threshold of acceptability to consumers and manufacturers.

Now that you have an overall picture of the sub-revolutions and laws that impact the world of information technology, let's delve more deeply into the underlying structure.

# Chapter 2: Making Sense of Layers

**Information Technology** is the people, processes, software, and hardware that make up the information flow in the operations of an organization. Information technology is "layered", like the skins of an onion. Knowing which layer you are on is essential to knowing which type of information technology is being talked about. This chapter will introduce the concept of a technology map and give an overview of each layer. It will also describe some of the basic "laws" (actually rules of thumb) that govern the world of information technology. The following chapters will delve into the details of each layer: Software, Hardware, and Networking.

## Why You Need to Understand the Layers

Businesses started using computers in the 60s and 70s - large, multi-million dollar mainframe computers that took a staff of people to manage and program and special rooms to house. Only technical people understood what was going on; business people were kept out of the "glass house". They could see what was going on and the result, but they weren't invited behind the wall.

Everything was owned and controlled at the same level; there weren't any layers. When a business invested in a computer, it bought the hardware, operating system software, specialized software, development software, programming, and maintenance services all from the same company for one price.

However, when personal computers became popular and networking became feasible, it was a different world. In this world products and services came from dozens of different vendors who worked independently. Large technology firms like IBM and AT&T were being broken up and forced to "unbundle" their products and services. The main purpose behind the regulations was to encourage competition and innovation, which indeed seems to have worked since innovation became the name of the game in business. However, the result is a compendium of vendors for a compendium of products that don't always work together as well as they should. Therefore, for businesses to get the most value from IT, business people much understand the different components and how they fit together. To traverse this difficult terrain, business people need a technology map.

A *technology map* is a mental map of how technology works—how the different components of the systems in a business fit together. The map gives us a good understanding of how technology interacts. The map demonstrates the layering effect of IT.

The basic categories are shown in Table 1  shows categories that might be included in a technology map and examples of each category.  In reality, a technology map is not generic, but must be documented for each individual company with the people, process, hardware, software, and networking installed at that company.  This introductory guide will deal exclusively with the computer hardware, software, and networking layers. (The People and Process levels are covered in detail in the book *Entrepreneur's Guide to Managing Information Technology.)*

## Software

Chapter 2 covers software, which is always *on top* of hardware. Software is ephemeral; the instructions for the hardware.  It can't really be seen, felt, or touched because it is composed of binary code stored on a disc. There are five different types of software:

- ◆ Application
- ◆ Specialized
- ◆ Development
- ◆ Utilities
- ◆ Operating System

Each category of software will be explained in more detail in the next chapter.

## Hardware

Hardware is what you see when you look at a computer. Hardware can be categorized as a *main* or *peripheral* component. There are also different types:

- ◆ Microcomputers (or personal computers),
- ◆ Workstations (a more powerful device than a personal computer),
- ◆ Servers (also called minicomputers or midrange computers),
- ◆ Mainframes (and supercomputers).

Hardware will be explained in more detail in Chapter 3.

**Table 1 Technology Map Basic Categories**

| MAJOR | MINOR | CATEGORIES |
|---|---|---|
| People | Ability | Hi Ability, Low Experience |
| | | Low Ability , Hi Experience |
| | Experience | Hi Ability, Hi Experience |
| | | Low Ability , Low Experience |
| Process | Who (Role) | Flow charts and process documentation – often obtained by watching people and what they do as well as asking them. |
| | What (Task) | |
| | When (Prompt or Time) | |
| Software | Application | Wordprocessing (Word, WordPerfect, MacWrite) |
| | | Spreadsheet (Excel, Lotus 123, Quattro Pro) |
| | | Database (DB2, Oracle, Sybase, MySQL, .PostgreSQL, SQL, Progress, Access, DBASE, Foxpro, Alpha4,  Filemaker) |
| | | Presentation/Graphics (Powerpoint, Illustrator, Corel Draw, Flash,Paint) |
| | | Email (Outlook/Exchange, Notes/Domino, Thunderbird) |
| | | Collaboration: (please see discussion for more details). |
| | Specialized | Financial: (Oracle, SAP, Macola, Business Dynamics, ACCPAC, Peach-tree, FAS, MAS90/200, Quickbooks, Quicken, Money, etc.) |
| | | CAD/CAM (Computer Aided Design/Manufacturing) AutoCAD, TurboCAD, |
| | | Vertical Market (Medical, Attorney, Retail, etc.) |
| | | Publishing (Quark, Microsoft Publisher, Adobe InDesign)) |

| MAJOR | MINOR | CATEGORIES |
|---|---|---|
| Software | Development | Languages -(Java, C, Cobol, Pascal, Perl, Visual Basic, etc.) |
| | Utilities | Workbenches & Middleware (Cold Fusion, PHP, Websphere, CASE Tools, Javascript, VBS, ASP, etc.) |
| | | Enterprise Network Management (OpenNMS, ENMS, HP Openview), Backup (Genie, Acronis, NTI, GRBackpro, Paragon, Veritas, NovaBackup) Firewall (SMS, Checkpoint, PICS) AntiVirus (Norton's Antivirus, McAfee, AVG, TrendMicro) |
| | Operating System | Single User (Vista, XP, Mac OS, Windows 95, 98, ME, 2000, DOS, etc.) |
| | | Multi User (Windows NT, 2000, 2003, or 2008; Novell Netware; Unix [Linux, AIX, Solaris, HPUX], AS/400, MVS, VSE) |
| Hardware | Main | CPU, Hard Drive, RAM, ROM, BIOS Chip; (Manufacturers: Dell, Gateway, IBM, HP, Honeywell, Unisys, etc.) |
| | Peripherals | Mouse, Keyboard, Monitor, Scanner, Camera, Printer, Flash Drive,etc. |
| Network | Network Applications | Client Browser (Explorer, Firefox, Safari) |
| | | Application servers (Progress, Orian, Jboss, Sun One, Enhydra, etc.) |
| | | Webservers (Apache, IIS, iPlanet) |
| | Internet Communication Protocols | TCP/IP, IPX/SPX, UPC, NetBIOS |
| | Network Interface | Hubs, Routers, Switches, and Network Interface Cards: (Ethernet, Token Ring) |
| | | Connection Type: Point to point leased line (T-1,T-3), Frame Relay, Satellite, FiOS, DSL, Cable Modem, Dialup |

# Network

Networking is the method of sharing data between two different computers. Although it contains within it both software (Network Applications and Internet Communication Protocols) and hardware (Network Interface), it sits *underneath* the computer hardware you normally associate with a computer or a server.

We will discuss the concept of the network in detail in two different chapters Chapter 3 is on Internetworking. We will discuss the protocols and applications of the Internet and the World Wide Web. Chapter 4 will be on networking, will delve into the physical networking of local area networks and wide area networks.

## In Between Categories: Firmware

Although there is no category for it in the technology map, mention must be made of a device that comes in between hardware and software called *firmware*. Sometimes instructions get "burned" into the circuitry of a component – like a chip. Then it's not really hardware, but it's not really software, either, so we call it firmware. Your computer has software called BIOS (basic input/output software), but instead of being stored on the hard drive like all the other operating system software, the BIOS software is stored on a ROM chip inside your computer. The software is stored in CMOS (complementary metal-oxide semiconductor) which doesn't take much power. Inside your PC is a tiny battery attached to the ROM chip so that it doesn't forget how to boot up (turn on). But the battery lasts for years. Most computers are obsolete years before the battery runs out.

Most peripheral devices have some sort of firmware inside them. Every cell phone, every camera, every device that connects to a computer has a chip in it that cannot be categorized either as hardware or software. Even your car has firmware – a computer controlled ignition device is really just a firmware card. For many years, General Motors was the #1 producer of computing devices in the world because each car they sold had a firmware chip inside that provided the instructions.

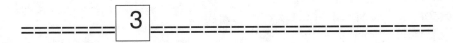

# Chapter 3: Software

Software is anything that is considered an instruction for the computer. You can't necessarily see it or touch it like you can hardware. It is generally in digital format, except when someone prints out the code. Even then – what you are seeing is a representation of the software – not the software itself.

Software breaks down into a couple of useful categories;

- Application
- Specialized
- Development
- Utilities
- Operating System

## Application Software

**Application** software is the general purpose software that you would see and use everyday. General application software is like multi-purpose rooms; it provides a basic configuration or design for doing something, but the actual content and structure is left up to the user. The main types of general application software are used in offices and homes for a variety of computer tasks. Application software is categorized by its purpose; wordprocessing, spreadsheet, presentation, email, collaboration, financial.

### *Wordprocessing*

A Wordprocessor is used to write letters and documents - the equivalent of a computerized typewriter (and no one who has learned to use a wordprocessor has ever gone back to using a clunky typewriter, see Figure 1). In the early days of computing (the 80's and 90's) there were dozens of wordprocessing programs to choose from such as WordPerfect, Multimate, Displaywriter, WordStar, MacWrite, FullWrite, etc. These days, however, most people use Microsoft Word because it is WYSIWYG (What you see is what you get) and relatively easy to use.

**Figure 1  A Selectric typewriter circa 1980**

### *Spreadsheet*

The use of wordprocessing was actually secondary to the primary use of personal computers in the early days. The very first "application" available for personal computers was VisiCalc, a spreadsheet program , which sold for $99 in 1979 and ran on an Apple IIe computer (which cost about $1200, had no hard drive, and had 16k of memory.). A spreadsheet enabled accountants to stop poring over paper lists of numbers where one mistake could cause hours of rework. (See Figure 2.[14]) Instead, they could type those columns of numbers into cells and have them automatically sum. If one of the numbers changed, the sum would automatically change.

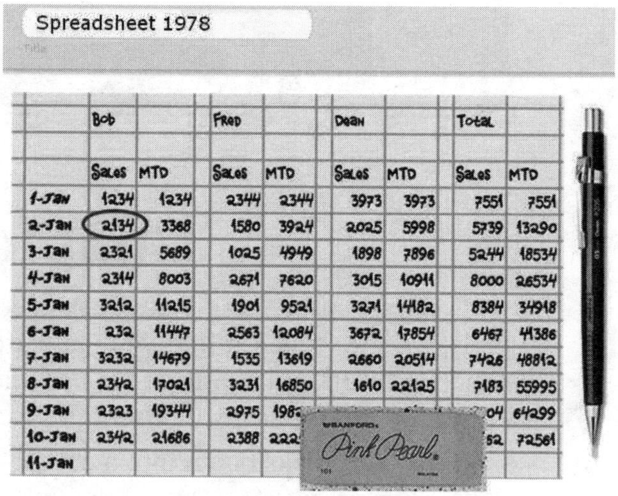

VisiCalc soon fell by the wayside as Lotus 123 became available on the IBM PC. Since IBM was the top mainframe computer vendor, they were already servicing all the large companies who were using mainframe computers, so they easily sold the personal computers and spreadsheets to the finance

**Figure 2  Manual Spreadsheet circa 1978**

divisions of those companies. Lotus 123 was followed quickly by Quattro Pro and Multiplan (which was eventually bought by Microsoft and became Excel, the most popular spreadsheet in use today).

## *Presentation/Graphics*

Although in the early early days application software was limited to just text, eventually some applications became available that could show pictures. Instead of laboring over transparencies or slide presentations, people realized they could connect the personal computer to a project and show presentations and graphics much more easily. Harvard Graphics was one of the first presentation packages for the PC, followed by the powerful Corel Draw. Both Harvard Graphics and Corel Draw fell by the wayside in a few years, however, as Microsoft released the easy-to-use Powerpoint program.

Although there aren't many competitors for Powerpoint for slide presentations, there are many programs available that do graphics. Graphics packages come in two different flavors: raster graphics or vector graphics. Raster graphics focuses on each individual bit and its color. Graphic programs that use raster graphics are Microsoft Paint, MacPaint, Photoshop, Paint Shop Pro, or iPhoto. Vector graphics, on the other hand, focus on objects rather than each individual bit. Vector graphics packages include Illustrator, Corel Draw, FireWorks, MacDraw, InkScape and DrawIt. More recent versions of some programs such as Paint Shop Pro and Adobe FireWorks include the capabilities of both raster graphics and vector graphics.

## *Database*

While it was possible to store lists of names and addresses in a wordprocessor or a spreadsheet, neither were well designed for the purpose of managing those names and addresses (or lists of anything else, either). The database programs became the fourth

---

[14] The graphic illustration of the manual spreadsheet is courtesy of Bill Jelen (aka "Mr. Excel") from http://www.mrexcel.com/tip076.shtml, originally published September 30, 2004 and accessed in May, 2008.

essential office application. Databases, however, by their very nature are a little more complicated than the other application software.

In the early days of mainframe computers, the data (such as customer names, addresses, inventory items, orders, etc.) was stored in proprietary formats on tapes. The programmer would write code that would store the data entered or retrieve the data that had already been stored. Files were "flat", without any relationships or hierarchies. The customer address file, for example, really had

> **Relative Complexity of Databases**
> Databases are much more complex than wordprocessors, spreadsheets, or presentation software, so it is quite a learning curve to use one. Most business leaders don't need to learn how to *create* databases - but they do need to learn how to query data from them and design reports for them. Business people should also understand which databases work with which types of hardware and which applications.

no relationship with the customer order file. The programmer would write code that would look up the customer address each time it was needed when reading the customer order, but there was no "connection" between them. *seperation of programs and data*

When databases moved to the personal computer world, a new paradigm for storing the data was developed called *relational database management.* Instead of needing a programmer to write code to look up the customer address each time it was needed, the two files were stored with a *key field* that would allow the two files to *relate*. Instead of relying upon programming code, the link to the customer address was imbedded in the customer order file. Relational databases drastically changed the way programs stored and retrieved data. The relationship could be set up at the beginning and the data could be accessed anytime without programming.

dBASE II, published by Ashton Tate, was the name of the first relationship database management program widely available for the PC. As it became more and more recognized as useful, hundreds of other database programs became available encompassing a range of needs from cheap and easy to highly complex, expensive and robust. Just to name a few of the databases available, there was Sybase, SQL, MySQL, .PostgreSQL, Progress, Ingres, Access, dBASE, rBase, Foxpro, Alpha4, Filemaker, Paradox, DataEase, ProFiler, Informix, Btrieve, Watcom, and Oracle. Instead of programming directly to store information, application programmers began building *on top of* these database programs, letting the database handle the actual file-open, write data, close file commands. While there has been a little bit of consolidation in the world of relational database management systems, there are still a number to choose from, but each has its strengths and weaknesses.

Access (by Microsoft) is probably the most common database available. It is generally easy to use (insofar as any database can be said to be easy to use. See inset: Relative Complexity of Databases.) Although easy to use, relatively inexpensive, and widely available, Access is not *robust.* Access databases often get corrupted or damaged so that they cannot be opened. It would not be wise to rely upon an Access database for business critical data. Additionally, Access should be limited to relatively small databases. If the database gets much beyond a 40 or 50 thousand records, it begins to get bogged down, slow, and more easily corrupted. Access is also not a very good choice if you plan on putting the data on a web server. While certainly possible to do, web applications based upon Access databases have a tendency to "break" frequently, requiring frequent reboots of the web server. Despite its drawbacks, for an office to keep track of names, addresses, inventory, or lists of any sort, Access is the best choice because it is inexpensive and relatively easy to use.

Microsoft also sells a more robust database, MS SQL, (usually pronounced Sequel although sometime people spell out the letters as in S Q L, standing for Structured Query Language. See the inset about multiple uses of the term SQL).

At the top of the spectrum is DB2, the only relational database management system that runs on large traditional mainframe computers (and the descendant of System/R). Like all mainframe software, DB2 requires dedicated programmers and is very expensive. It is only required for the largest systems and the largest databases, and is not easily utilized via the web.

> **Multiple uses of the term: SQL**
> One common point of confusion is that Microsoft sells a particular database called SQL, but the letters SQL also refer to a generic language developed in the 70s for IBM's relational database system (called System/R at the time) which was short for SEQUEL (Structured English QUery Language). The query language called SQL is used with ALL relational database management systems, not just those with SQL in the name.

Oracle is the top database for both robustness and volume. Oracle can handle millions of records with ease, and hundreds of people accessing the data at the same time. Oracle doesn't get corrupt easily. However, Oracle is expensive and requires dedicated staff to install and maintain the database. It runs best on server systems running one of the Unix-based operating systems. (Operating systems are discussed in more detail later.)

For systems that require web access, the top choice is MySQL. Most web hosting services include a copy of MySQL already set up and configured for use on the website. A particular web programmer may prefer PostgreSQL (which is also Open Source), but that is not included for free as often as MySQL.

There are some industries that have had so many systems developed with legacy databases that they must still be maintained (though when developing a new system, few programmers would want to work in them as they don't have all the new features of web accessible databases.) One such database is Sybase, which was often used in financial firms on Wall Street. Progress was often used in the construction industry. Informix was a top choice in Retail.

> **Open Source Applications**
> MySQL is an example of an **open source** application. **Open Source** is a movement among programmers who felt that corporations who charged money for software were unfair. In the Open Source movement, programmers volunteer their time to develop and maintain software for each other to use without paying anything. In other words, the cost to use MySQL is nothing (if you don't count the cost of the labor in setting up MySQL). Anyone (who has the technical expertise to do so) can download MySQL and set it up on a website. Open Office is a free downloadable wordprocessor and spreadsheet program, Opera is a free downloadable web browser, Linux is a free downloadable operating system and Apache is a free downloadable web server.

## Email

In the early days of computers, a corporation would install an email system so that employees could send messages to each other. It wasn't until the Internet that employees of one company could send email messages to an employee of another company. Today, of course, email is  ubiquitous. For many businesses, it is as hard to imagine doing business without email as it would be to run a business without telephones. But email is still a relatively recent process. In 2003, a survey of 268 businesses revealed that 35% still did not have Internet email (although 27% of them had corporate email within the company). Almost eight percent did not have any email at all. The graph is shown in Figure 3.

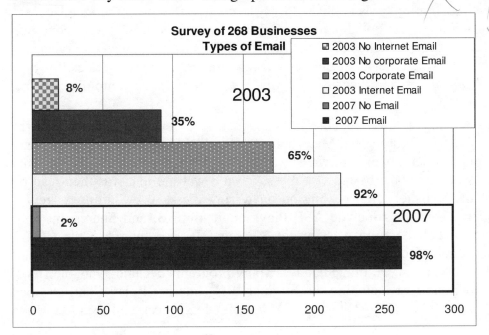

**Figure 3 Survey of Types of Email**[15]

Even in companies that had email, not everyone got an email address. Only 50% of the companies gave the majority of their employees email addresses, as can be seen in Figure 4. The same survey done just four years later showed that 98% of the companies had Internet email, and most gave email addresses to all of their employees.

More detailed discussion of how email is used can be found in the Email section of the chapter on Internetworking.

*Collaboration*

The term *Collaboration Software* has been applied to systems that are designed to enable groups of people to work together "virtually". Collaboration software is also

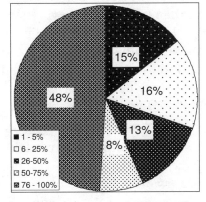

**Figure 4    Survey of Employee Percentages with Email in 2003**[14]

often called workgroup software, or knowledge management software. The field is so new that the terms, categories, features and functions are changing at an extremely rapid pace, so whatever is written here will likely be out of date by the time you read it.

---

[15] Courtesy of ETM Associates, Inc in conjunction with Berks County Chamber of Commerce. Used by permission.

Collaboration started with a simple add-on to email; shared folders. Exchange and Domino (the server portion of the Outlook and Notes email client/server systems) added a shared folders feature that enabled people logged into the system to place or retrieve files so that people didn't have to attach files to email messages in order to share information. Groove and Sharepoint are both collaboration tools published by Microsoft that expand the "file sharing" concept and try to catch up to the collaboration capabilities of the Notes/Domino combination. Groove is peer to peer (which means it doesn't rely upon a centralized server) and Sharepoint is web-based (which means it runs on a centralized server). Sometimes this type of software is called *portal* software because it forms the "entryway" for employees to get into a corporate website.

Next came software that allowed people to manage lists of email addresses such as Listserv, Mailman, EzMLM, FutureQuest, Majordomo, or Phplist. Discussion group software (also known as forum or bulletin board software) was another way of collaboration. Discussion group software enabled people to "post" a message on a website that was then read by others who went to the website, often posting an answering message by hitting a "reply" button on the webpage. Examples include ASP Playground, PhpBB, and Sharepoint software. Another aspect of collaboration was Instant Message (IM) or Internet Chat (IC), a method of synchronous communication where people can talk with each other by typing lines into a dialog box that others can see immediately. Many programs became available (most for free) to allow people to chat including the original IRQ (Internet Relay Chat, an open source program), Yahoo Messenger, AIM (for AOL Instant Messenger), and Windows Live Messenger.

Many people consider teleconferencing or bridge calling a Collaboration technology that uses special software. With teleconferencing, many people call the same number and everyone can talk and hear everyone else at the same time. With the addition of a microphone and speakers, people can use their computer like a phone, calling up other people (even regular phones) with special software and services such as Skype and Globe7 and Packetel. With the addition of a webcam (a small low-quality video camera attached as a peripheral to your computer) people can talk with each other face to face in a live video conference called a Webconference. Larger groups can meet over the Internet using webconferencing software such as WebEX, NetMeeting or Packetel.

Some companies are attempting to package many of these independent components together in order to provide more features and functions. Yahoo Groups, Topica, and Google Groups provide some of the functionality of Groove, Sharepoint, and Domino such as shared file space, instant messaging, listserv, even webconferencing.

Related to group sites are *weblogs* or just *blogs* for short. A blog is a site where someone posts articles or opinions in a frequent basis, inviting others to comment on their posts. Topsites.blogflux.com is an aggregator site and, at the time of this writing, contained over one hundred thousand other blogs. Additionally, most newspapers, magazines, and news media have added blogging as one of their tools for getting and keeping readers.

Social networking is another form of collaboration software, albeit web based and not targetted for small groups but rather for growing users in the millions. Social Networking sites encourage virtual communities by allowing individuals to post information about themselves, and then invite other people they know to connect to their on-line profile. LinkedIn.com is a business networking site. MySpace.com, and Facebook.com have younger clientele and are more about social networking than business networking. Virtual sites like SecondLife.com are a spinoff from multi-user fantasy games but focus more on living virtually than playing games.

Collaboration on-line has reached new heights with software available on certain web-sites known as *wikis.* The popularization of wiki software started with Wikipedia.org, a free world-wide encyclopedia that anyone in the world can edit. Rather than the chaos some people envisioned, wikipedia instead proved itself to be highly structure and relatively accurate, with the advantage of being able to adapt to new information much more rapidly than any printed encyclopedia. The model proved that huge numbers of people can collaborate effectively on world-wide projects. Started in January of 2001, wikipedia has grown to over ten million articles in over 250 languages.

Collaboration tools and methods continue to change on a frequent basis, but eventually the novelty of each new innovation will pass and people will tend to continue those which provide the most value and drop those that don't.

# Specialized Software

Specialized software are programs that have been developed for a specific purpose or a specific industry. Specialized software can run on a PC, a server, or a mainframe computer. We will discuss three types of specialized software; financial, CAD/CAM, vertical industry, and publishing.

## *Financial*

Financial software is of special interest to people in business. Financial software has been developed to track all the financial transactions of a person or company. Programs like Microsoft Money or Intuit Quicken are used by individuals to track their income and expenses. Over recent years these packages have morphed into a front end for banking and investments, connecting directly with financial institutions so that people don't need to enter their transactions, but rather download them automatically from the website. They also contain reports to calculate net worth and graph expenses.

Corporations need more sophisticated financial software than individuals. One difference between corporate financial software and individual financial software is the ability to do "accrual" accounting. Individuals use "cash" accounting; income is recorded when the check is deposited and expenses are recorded when the check is written. Accrual accounting identifies more specifically exactly when transactions can be recorded as income, expenses, assets or liabilities, and follow rules known as GAAP (Generally Accepted Accounting Principals).

In accrual accounting, in addition to recording income and expenses, companies need to record accounts payable (money that needs to be paid in the future) and accounts receivable (money that will be received in the future), as well as assets (building and equipment owned by the company), liabilities (money borrowed that must be paid back) and equity (how much the investors in the business have contributed to the value of the business).

Over the years, the purpose of financial software has changed. Initially financial software focused on the general ledger and was known as accounting software. In time, however, modules were added for all the other functions of a business that required transactions that eventually posted to the general ledger. Along with the concept that the financial software could help leaders of an organization plan an manage the organization came a new term; Enterprise Resource Planning (ERP). Initially focused only on huge corporations, the functionality of ERP has reached down into even the financial software used by the smallest companies. ERP systems generally have multiple modules available so that corporations that use them can identify specifically which modules they wish to use. A list of almost one hundred modules available for a variety of popular financial packages is listed in Table 2. The more common modules such as General Ledger (GP), Accounts Payable (AP), Accounts Receivable (AR), Sales Orders (SO), Purchase Orders (PO) and Human Resources (HR) are often found in all the financial packages, whereas the rest of the modules may or may not be available with that particular ERP system.

The combination of modules is designed to span the entire *supply chain.* The term "supply chain management" was coined by Keith Oliver, a Booz Allen Hamilton executive in the early eighties, but it has grown to encompass an entire field made possible by ERP systems. Prior to ERP systems, most departments and divisions of corporations each used a different type of software, and rarely did the systems link or share information. The list of orders was in one system, the list of items in another system, the list of items shipped in another system, the invoice sent in another system, the checks received in another system, and the posting to the general ledger that fed the quarterly reports was in yet another system. Many of these "systems" were not even computerized, but rather manual systems. Most of the time transferring data from one system to another was also manual, and therefore fraught with errors and inaccuracies.

Although initially ERP systems also did not link different modules together (some are still that way, oddly enough), for the most part ERP systems served to combine all the information so that corporate leaders could review information about their company from *end to end.* The links of these different aspects (marketing, sales, operations/manufacturing, delivery, invoicing, and payment) are considered links in the supply chain.

In the early days of computers there were hundreds of financial software vendors, but a great deal of consolidation has occurred. Now there are only a handful (although many of them still have programs used by the customers of the packages they acquired since changing financial packages is not very easy to do.) A list of all the software packages and their current owners can be found on Ned Lilly's website http://www.erpgraveyard.com/tombs.html, the first page of the May, 2008 version is shown in Figure 5.

**Table 2 Financial Software Modules List**

| | | |
|---|---|---|
| General Ledger | Report Writer | Sales Forecasting |
| Accounts Receivable | Business Partners Mngmnt | Quality Management |
| Accounts Payable | Advanced Planning | Shipping and Receiving |
| Sales Orders | Advanced Reports | Shop Floor Data Collection |
| Purchase Order | Advanced Scheduling | StarShip Link |
| Purchasing | Business Intelligence & Reporting (Analytics) | Strategic Decisions |
| Payroll | Bank transactions | Supply Chain Management |
| Human Resources | Bar Code Reader | Synchronizer Foundation |
| Financial Management | Budgeting / Cash Flow | TimeCards |
| Bill of Material | Business Insights | Tracking Material Lots |
| Material Requirements | Capable to Promise | Visual Integrator |
| Bank Reconciliation | Collaborative Workspace | Sales Opportunity Mngmnt |
| Warehouse Management | Config & Development | Notifying Employees |
| Fast Forms | Creating Routings | Work Order |
| Customer Relationship Management (CRM) | Job Orders & Job Costs | Magnetic Media Reporting |
| Customer Service | Inventory Control | Manufacturing |
| Demand Forecasting | Business Alerts | Materials Management |
| e-Business Manager | Service Management | Mobile Manager |
| Engineering | Inventory Management | Monitoring Metrics |
| Events and Actions | Return Merchandise Authorization | Quoting and Estimating |
| Exploring Operations | Hosting Services: inquiry | Multi-Dimension Inventory |
| Fixed Asset Accounting | Hosting Services: order | Outlook Integration |
| Sales Forecaster | Hosting Services: store | Product Configurator |
| Customer Order Management | Sales and Distribution | Production Management |
| Credit Card Processing | | Progress Billing |
| | | Project Accounting Software |
| | | Monitoring Production |
| | | Logistics |

**The ERP Graveyard Scorecard (first page only)**

*Scorecard key: Number of bells refers to the number of times a product or company has been acquired. (The original ERP Graveyard shows tombstones, but they did not reproduce well, so bells were substituted - as in "The Bell tolls for thee." Additionally, this is just the first page - more can be found on http://www.erpgraveyard.com/tombs.html)*

### Tier 1: The Twin Titans

**Oracle**
- 🔔 Hyperion
- 🔔 Siebel
- 🔔 Retek
- 🔔 Demantra
- 🔔 PeopleSoft
- 🔔🔔 JDEdwards
- 🔔🔔 YouCentric
- 🔔🔔🔔 Numetrix
- 🔔🔔 Vantive
- 🔔🔔 RedPepper
- 🔔 Datalogix
- 🔔 G-Log

**SAP**
- 🔔 OutlookSoft
- 🔔 Triversity
- 🔔 TopTier
- 🔔 Top Manage (now B1)
- 🔔 Lighthammer

### Tier 2: Infor and the Infor-bait

**Infor Global**
- 🔔 Former SSA Apps
- 🔔🔔 Provia
- 🔔🔔 Former CA Apps (InterBiz)
- 🔔🔔🔔 MK
- 🔔🔔🔔🔔 PRMS
- 🔔🔔🔔 Data3
- 🔔🔔🔔 Acacia
- 🔔🔔🔔🔔 Ask
- 🔔🔔 Former Invensys Apps
- 🔔🔔🔔 Baan
- 🔔🔔🔔🔔 CAPS Logistics
- 🔔🔔🔔 Marcam
- 🔔🔔🔔🔔 MXP
- 🔔🔔 Infinium (fka Software2000)
- 🔔🔔 E-piphany
- 🔔🔔 Boniva
- 🔔🔔 Arzoon
- 🔔🔔 EXE
- 🔔🔔 Ironside Technologies
- 🔔🔔 BPCS
- 🔔 Mapics
- 🔔🔔 Frontstep (fka SYMIX)
- 🔔🔔🔔 Frontstep Planning
- 🔔🔔 Pivotpoint (fka Spectrum)
- 🔔🔔🔔 Growthpower
- 🔔🔔🔔 Minxware
- 🔔🔔🔔 Maincor
- 🔔🔔🔔 Thru-Put
- 🔔 Infor
- 🔔 Mercia
- 🔔 Varial
- 🔔🔔 Swan
- 🔔 SCT Adage
- 🔔🔔 Fygir
- 🔔 Lilly
- 🔔 Aperum
- 🔔 FACTS
- 🔔 TakeStock
- 🔔🔔 DMAS
- 🔔 Brain
- 🔔 NxTrend
- 🔔🔔 Dimasys
- 🔔 daly.commerce
- 🔔 Formation
- 🔔 IncoDev

### Tier 3: SMB and Below!

**Microsoft Business Dynamics**
- 🔔 Great Plains
- 🔔🔔 Real World
- 🔔🔔 Solomon
- 🔔🔔 FRX
- 🔔 Navision
- 🔔🔔 Damgaard/Axapta

**Sage**
- 🔔 Abra
- 🔔 ACCPAC
- 🔔🔔 SBT
- 🔔 ACT!
- 🔔 Adonix
- 🔔 Best
- 🔔 BusinessVision
- 🔔 BusinessWorks
- 🔔 FAS
- 🔔 MAS90/200
- 🔔 Peachtree
- 🔔🔔🔔 PFW (formerly Platinum)
- 🔔 SalesLogix
- 🔔 SimplyAccounting
- 🔔 Tetra
- 🔔 Timberline

**Consona**
- 🔔 Made2Manage
- 🔔 Capri
- 🔔 DTR
- 🔔 ADS
- 🔔 Cimnet
- 🔔 AXIS
- 🔔 Encompix
- 🔔 Onyx
- 🔔 Intuitive
- 🔔🔔 SupplyWorks
- 🔔🔔 Relevant (INFIMACS)

**Exact**
- 🔔 Macola
- 🔔 Kewill ERP
- 🔔🔔 Alliance/MFG
- 🔔🔔 MAX
- 🔔🔔 JobBOSS
- 🔔 Vanguard

**Figure 5  Evidence of Financial Software Consolidation: the ERP Graveyard**

As can be seen from the graph in Figure 6, very large companies usually have a financial package from either SAP or Oracle. Medium or large companies usually have a financial package from either Microsoft or Sage. The most popular software for small companies is Intuit's Quickbooks.

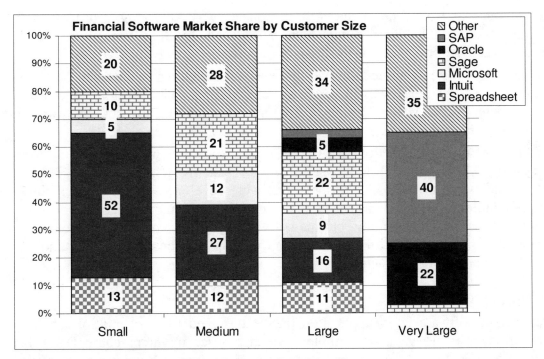

**Figure 6 Financial Software Market Share by Customer Size**

Almost all financial software is built on top of a database, so often in addition to choosing the financial software, a company can also choose to run the software on either Oracle, Sybase, SQL, or DB2 database. Additionally, though most software had add-on portals that allow employees to enter transactions from the web (and/or a module that will do E-commerce so that the company can sell directly over the web), they almost all run as client-server systems instead of distributed transaction system[16]s.

Financial software for larger companies do not really exist as "off the shelf" packages. Rather, large companies purchase the software "by the seat" (as if it were off the shelf), but are actually purchasing the development time of the consultants who "customize" the package. Systems like SAP, JD Edwards, Hyperion, Oracle Financials, and PeopleSoft are actually closer to development environments than already programmed software packages, (Development packages are discussed in the next section.)

## CAD/CAM Software

In addition to financial software, many businesses started using software that was specifically developed to design and manufacture products, interfacing with the robotics or equipment on the factory floor. These systems are called Computer Aided Design (CAD) or Computer Aided Engineering (CAE) systems, In the days of the mainframe, large companies such as General Motors (GM) and Lockheed had dedicated computers with proprietary software to help engineers design. But when microcomputers started to proliferate, the

---

[16] Client server systems require a fast persistant network connection, whereas distributed transaction systems can be done over a slower, intermittant connection.

capabilities migrated as well. One of the earliest pioneers was AutoCAD, a program published by AutoDesk in 1982, followed within the next decade by SolidWorks published by Dessault Systems and TurboCAD by IMSI/Design.

CAD systems initially just printed out two-dimensional blueprints or drawings on a large plotter. However, as the field evolved, CAD systems went to 3 dimensions, and started linking to Computer Aided Manufacturing (CAM) systems that actually cut, bent, or connected materials in order to manufacture the finished product.

One of the most recent innovations for CAD/CAM is to link them with Building Management Systems (BMS) or Building Automation Systems (BAS). The Building Management systems can use the CAD designs that were developed as part of the architectural design of a building in order to manage the heat, light, air conditioning, plumbing, etc. BMS systems are just now developing, but the software is mostly coming from companies that manufacturer sensors and controls like Johnson Controls, Siemens Building Technology, Delta, Distech, Circon and KMC controls.

## Vertical Market Software

Vertical market software is an application that is designed to meet multiple software needs of a particular industry. For example, a dentist office might purchase DentiMax, StarByte Dental or EasyDental. An insurance agent might purchase Your Insurance Office, and a Massage Therapist might purchase Your Massage Office. Generally these packages include a scheduling program, a wordprocessor, a customer database, a human resources module, and financial software. For someone who has limited experience with computers, these integrated packages can help automate simple office tasks very easily and provide much-needed technical support.

As more and more people become familiar with general use programs such as Microsoft Office, however, vertical market software has been decreasing in popularity due to the high cost and limited capabilities.

## Publishing

Publishing software is a little different from other general use office software for a number of reasons. For one, publishing is one of the few industries where the Macintosh computer has held a very strong niche. For another, it is deceptively difficult to combine text and graphics on paper or on the computer screen despite the many years that people have been doing it.

Publishing software sometimes gets lumped into other categories such as wordprocessing (like Word and Wordperfect) and/or graphics design (like Illustrator and/or Corel Draw) or programs that publish in standard format such as Macromedia Flash or Acrobat Writer. But publishing, most especially Desktop Publishing (DTP) (a term coined by Adobe, the publisher of the original DTP package Pagemaker) is limited to laying out on a printed page or a computer screen the graphics and the text. Generally, the text is still written with a wordprocessor and the graphics is still designed in a graphics package. Additionally, the final product is still actually "published" by another program like Flash or Acrobat. The publishing software deals with issues such as headers, footers, stories continuing on other pages, hyphenation, placement of graphics, etc.

The top publishing program in the field of print publishing is Quark, which still runs on a Macintosh computer. Microsoft also sells Microsoft Publisher and it is still possible to purchase Adobe Pagemaker (for either the Macintosh or Windows) and Corel Ventura.

There are many contenders for web publishing, the two most popular are Adobe InDesign (formerly called DreamWeaver) and Microsoft Expressions (formerly called Frontpage).

# Development Software

Of all the categories of software, development software has changed the most over the course of the past thirty years. Development software includes programming languages and development tools (also known as workbenches or middleware) that enable programmers to write code so that other people can use the software that results.

## *Languages*

Programming languages is the "code" that developers write in so that computers can understand the instructions. Languages can be categorized in "generations", and is often abbreviated as 1GL, 2GL, 3GL, 4GL, or 5GL with GL standing for generation language.

The first generation (1GL) of computer coding was machine language or binary code. A computer can, at its very core, only understand two things; on or off (or 1 or 0). In general, people don't program in machine language.

The second generation (2GL) was composed of short commands that represented a series of binary codes. This was often called assembler or assembly language, and only the very earliest programmers coded in it. Assembler language only works for the one specific configuration of hardware for which it was developed.

The third generation (3GL) was the first higher level of programming, the "real" programming language. Third generation programs could be written with any text editor, but then were *compiled* by a program that would take the text and convert it from the programming language into machine code. Examples include PL/I, C, C+, C# (pronounced C-sharp), Fortran, Perl, Cobol, Java, and BASIC. It takes considerable knowledge and talent to learn a programming language and is not something non-programmers can do easily.

The fourth generation (4GL) were designed to be easier to use, opening up development to the typical computer user rather than just dedicated programmers. Often 4GL's directly managed a relational database and contained english-like commands. Examples include dBASE, RBase, XBase, RPG, Informix, SQL, Focus, Mapper, Mark-IV, Progress, Ramis, Powerbuilder, Dataflex, Forte. Additionally, fourth generation languages were often *interpreted* instead of compiled. They required a program on the user's machine that would read and convert the code instantaneously instead of requiring the programmer to convert the code to machine language. This was a big deal because programs written with compiled languages could only be run on the type of computer for which it was compiled, whereas interpreted languages could run the same program on many different computers, relying upon the interpreter to feed the right machine language to the processor.

When they were first introduced, fifth generation languages (5GL) were touted as the next level of artificial intelligence - with the ability to understand natural language and learn through the use of a sophisticated set of conditional commands called a *neural network*. Examples included Logo, OOPS, LISP, and Smalltalk. When it became obvious that computers were still decades away from understanding natural language, fifth generation languages became the *object oriented* forms of traditional programming languages. Object oriented programming came about as a natural evolution from the text-based user interface of DOS and Unix to the menu and icon driven user interface of Windows and Macintosh computers. Visual BASIC (also known as VB.net), Object Pascal, Tuple, Python, C++, Rational Rose, and many others. Like third generation languages, programming in a 5GL is not for the average business person, but requires years of learning.

## *Development Tools*

In and around the programming languages themselves are many other "tools" that are necessary to turn the code into usable programs. The earliest of these simply partnered a text editor with a compiler so that developers didn't need to exit out of the text editor in order to compile and run the program. As software development became more sophisticated, more capabilities were added into the development environment.

> **Multiple Uses of Program**
>
> Another common point of confusion is the term *program* which can be used as a noun (as in "I want to purchase that software program") or as a verb (as in "Please progam the system to ask this question"). Programmers program progams is a grammatically correct sentence.
>
> Furthermore, *to program* generally means *to write code in a computer language*. In recent years, due to the proliferation of sophisticated workbenches and integrated development environments, programmers are often called *developers* because they don't actually write code anymore; they develop programs instead.

Many of these development tools require the use of a powerful workstation and a specialized development network environment. The first of these development systems was called a CASE workstation, and was touted specifically to develop client-server software. CASE stands for Computer-Aided Software Engineering. Typically these systems included, in addition to the text editor and the compiler, a front-end system that helped the developer to envision the application. The developer would use the front end to design the underlying database, plan the screens and menus, and write the reports. Then, instead of typing thousands of lines of code, the developer would have the workstation program the code.

Next, these environments were called IDE, or Integrated Development Environments. IDEs sometimes included the same automation of CASE tools, but had to go one step further. While CASE tools were used to develop client-server systems designed to run on local area networks within a single building (which meant very fast connection speeds), IDEs expanded to include *middleware* and other items necessary for developing in a distributed environment over the wide area network[17]. Middleware was the name given to the "missing piece" between the different software components running on different machines in a distributed environment. For example, a relational database running on a dedicated database server

---

[17] More details about both local area networks and wide area networks can be found in the Networks chapter.

(such as SQL, Oracle, Sybase, or DB2) may need to connect to the application running on the application server written in a programming language (such as Visual Basic, Cobol, Java, or C). Since programming languages had no built-in commands to work with relational databases, another piece of programming was needed to enable them to work together. Examples of middleware include PHP, ASP/VBScript, ColdFusion, Perl, PHP, and Webmethods. [There are some who argue that JAVA, though starting as a programming language has evolved into middleware[18] because the Enterprise Edition of Java includes Remote Procedure Calls (RPC), Transaction Processing Monitors (TPM), Message Oriented Middleware (MOM), and Object Request Brokers (ORB), but most people consider Java a language, not a middleware.]

Starting in late 2007, a new term began to be used for these integrated environments; Application Lifecycle Management, or ALM. In addition to the software used directly by the developers for writing code, ALM systems include programs to help with change management, project management, requirements development, documentation development, testing, and quality assurance/defect tracking. A detailed list of ALM software can be found in Table 3.

## Utilities

In order to keep software and hardware working at peak efficiency and safety, sometimes we need additional software that doesn't directly do anything for us as users, but helps keep the computer or data safe and running. One problem with the Utility category is that over time needed utilities tend to be absorbed into the operation system and are no longer necessary as separate programs, so it is a difficult category to define.

In the early days of computing (when DOS was the top operating system) many people purchased third-party programs such as Norton's Utilities. These programs provided an easy-to-use file manager, a program to do back ups, and a program to undelete deleted files. When Windows 3.1 was released, however, it included a file manager and a back up utility. When Windows XP was released, it included a trash bin that could undelete files.

The Internet was developed without any built-in security. Instead, security was provided through the use of a *firewall,* a program that would only allow traffic through if it came from certain trusted addresses. To prevent issues a savvy user downloaded Black Ice or Zone Alarm onto their PCs. When Windows XP came out, however, it had a built-in firewall.

---

[18] Welsh, Tom. **Has Java become middleware?** *Middleware Spectra,* November 2000 http://www.middlewarespectra.com/abstracts/2000_11_06.htm, accessed May 17, 2008

**Table 3  Software tools in each category normally considered part of ALM**

**Integrated Application Lifecycle Management (ALM) Solutions**
- Borland ALM
- Jazz Team Concert
- Microsoft Visual Studio Team System
- Mylyn
- Rally Software
- Software Planning
- ThoughtWorks

**Change Management**
- Borland StarTeam
- CVS
- IBM Rational ClearCase
- Microsoft Visual Studio Team System
- Perforce
- Serena Dimensions
- Subversion

**Project Management**
- Achievo
- Artemis
- Borland Tempo
- Cranes InventX
- Fog Creek FogBugz
- IBM Rational Method Composer
- IBM Rational Portfolio Manager
- IBM Rational Team Unifying Platform
- Microsoft Project
- Microsoft Project Server
- Planisware OPX2
- Trac
- VertaBase

**Requirements Management**
- Borland Caliber
- Compuware Optimal Trace
- Goda Analyst Real Team System (ARTS)
- IBM Rational RequisitePro
- TechnoSolutions TopTeam
- Telelogic DOORS

**Build Management Systems**
- Apache Ant
- Apache Maven
- Borland Gauntlet
- CruiseControl
- IBM Rational Build Forge

**Testing Management**
- Borland SilkCentral Test Manager
- Compuware QADirector
- IBM Rational TestManager
- Mercury Test Director
- Traq QATraq

**Quality assurance/Defect Tracking**
- Atlassian JIRA
- Borland StarTeam
- Fog Creek FogBugz
- IBM Rational ClearQuest
- Mozilla Bugzilla
- Seapine TestTrack Pro
- Serena TeamTrack

Of course, there are many people who still purchase utilities such as file managers, backup programs, and firewalls because they do not like the software that comes with the operating system, or their needs go beyond the capabilities of the desktop version of the programs. For example, a corporation IT Manager trying to back up dozens of servers would have to purchase a dedicated backup system in order to manage the complexity. Someone who has to convert data frequently from one system to another might purchase a conversion utility.

Most people still purchase anti-virus utilities such as Norton's Antivirus or MacAfee's Antivirus. A virus is a program that is designed to do damage to your system by changing or deleting essential code needed for the system to run effectively. Another category of *malware* (software designed with malicious intent) is *spyware* - a program designed to watch what you do on your computer, including watching which websites you go to. Ostensibly designed to sell the information to marketing brokers, malware often slows down your computer to the point where it is unusable. For a few years, to eliminate spyware a computer user had to purchase both an anti-virus program and an anti-spyware program, but these days both utilities are included in the same software.

> In the early days, microcomputers could not connect to mainframe and minicomputer systems. Instead "dumb terminals" (a system with a keyboard and a monitor, but no internal processor, memory, or storage) were used to connect to the mainframe and minicomputers. The only way for a microcomputer to connect to them was to run software that emulated the "dumbness" of a terminal. This software was known as terminal emulation software.

## Operating System Software

The base software of any computer is the Operating System (OS). Without an OS, the computer makes a really good doorstop, but it can't do much else. The Operating System tells the computer what the keyboard is, what storage is, what memory is, how to display text and graphics on the monitor, how to get files, how to store them, etc. Oss can be categorized as multi-user or single user.

### Multi-user Operating Systems

Mainframe computers and servers were designed for hundreds of people to use them at the same time. Mainframes and servers usually come with a proprietary OS that does not work on any other hardware. For example, International Business Machines (IBM) sells an OS called **i** for its AS/400 lines. VSE & MVS are the OSs for IBM's mainframes. Hewlett Packard (HP) uses the MPE OS to run its HP3000 servers.

The story is a little more complicated when it comes to OSs that run on servers and microcomputers. In the early 80s, microcomputers were limited to one individual user. But as the need for connection between microcomputer grew, two OSs developed to fill the niche; AT&T's Unix and Novell's Netware.

Unix and Netware were not, technically, the same. Unix was a multi-user OS that enabled many different devices (including both terminals and microcomputers) to connect and share resources such as file storage and printing. Unix originated in Bell Labs at AT&T (see the story of Unix), but had morphed into dozens of proprietary OSs by hardware manufacturers. For example, AIX was sold by IBM for its RS/6000 models, Sun sells Solaris to run all its systems, and HPUX runs on HP workstations.

Novell Netware was a Network OS (NOS); a program designed to run on one microcomputer that enabled other microcomputers to connect and share resources such as file storage and printing. Netware could not connect to a terminal; it expected a microcomputer including its own storage, memory, and processing to connect.

In the late eighties and early nineties, IT people were usually strongly for either Unix or Netware. In 1993, however, a new kid appeared on the block from Microsoft: Windows NT.

Providing much of the same capability as both Unix and Netware, Windows NT had the added advantage of a graphical user interface, which made it much easier to learn to use than either of the alternatives. While growth for Windows NT was slower than end-user OSs and NT's reliability left much to be desired (requiring frequent reboots in order to avoid unexpected crashes), Microsoft NT eventually overtook Novell Netware (due in part to Novell's leadership getting distracted in an attempt at diversification by acquiring companies like WordPerfect and Corel trying to develop a suite of applications to compete with Microsoft's Office). By 1998 Windows NT was outselling Novell Netware.

Neither, however, were able to keep up with the sudden popularity of the combined flavors of Unix - especially when the open source (and therefore freely downloaded) version of Unix called Linux became widely available. Because the technologists building the Internet worked for the universities where Unix was the primary OS, the Internet protocols adopted many of the features of Unix systems. By the year 2000, Unix had nearly 40% of the market (with 24% of that being Linux), Windows NT and its upgrade Windows 2000 had 36%, and Novell Netware was down to 19%[19]. Most webservers on the World Wide Web running on the Internet today are Linux-based servers.

---

**The Story of Unix[20]**

Back in 1969, a couple of computer researchers, Ken Thompson and Dennis Ritchie, were working for AT&T (called Bell Labs at the time) on a computing project called MULTICS, (Multiplexed Information Computing System) with MIT (Massachusetts Institute of Technology) and Honeywell (part of General Electric at the time). Being very bright and relatively young, Ken and Dennis did not always spend all of their time doing boring programming work. To interject periods of fun, Ken utilized his abilities to write a multi-user computer game called Space Travel on the GE/Honeywell mainframe computer. The game was a simulation of the movement of the major bodies of the Solar System, with the players guiding a ship here and there, observing the scenery, and attempting to land on the various planets and moons - a very early rendition of today's simulation video games.

Unfortunately, the mainframe computer did not display the graphics very well, and movement was very jerky. Additionally, the cost of the timeshare for the mainframe was prohibitive; it cost about $75 to play a single game. So Ken found a castoff minicomputers (a DEC PDP-7), and Dennis helped him rewrite the game so that it would work on the PDP-7.

Things went well until AT&T decided to drop out of the joint project. Ken and Dennis were devastated; leaving the joint project would mean that access to the PDP-7 and the Space Travel game would be lost. The boys, however, did not want to give up their Space Travel game. So what did they do? Thinking quickly, (and with the help of J.F. Ossanna) they convinced AT&T to purchase a PDP-11 (ostensibly to write a word processing program) and wrote an entire OS as well as a C compiler so that they could port their game to the new computer!

Eventually they had to name the OS they wrote. Friend Brian Kernighan suggested the name "Unics" for Uniplexed Information Computing System (a pun; Unics was Multics without balls). Eventually the name was changed to Unix.

---

[19] O'Reilly, Tim. ***Linux/UNIX Server Market Share Beats NT/Win2K*** written on August 9, 2000 http://www.oreillynet.com/manila/tim/stories/storyReader$56. Accessed on May 18, 2008.

[20] Most of this story was documented on ***History and Timeline***, by the Open Group at http://www.unix.org/what_is_unix/history_timeline.html (Last updated on January 29, 2003, accessed on May 10, 2008) and on ***The Evolution of the Unix Time-sharing System*** by Dennis Ritchie at http://cm.bell-labs.com/cm/cs/who/dmr/hist.html (last published *AT&T Bell Laboratories Technical Journal 63 No. 6 Part 2, October 1984, pp. 1577-93.* )accessed on May 10, 2008).

---

**More About Unix**

Many people think that Unix is an acronym since it is often spelled in all caps UNIX. However, Unix is not an acronym. The reason it is spelled in all caps was that those early documenters were thrilled with the ability to use small caps in their very rudimentary wordprocessor, so they used UNIX in the documentation. Properly, it is Unix, although some developers consider **UNIX** the specific operating system developed in the seventies and **Unix** is used to refer to all the flavors of Unix that have evolved out of that original operating system.

Ken and Ritchie, of course, wrote Unix as employees of AT&T, so AT&T owned it. But US trade restrictions prevented AT&T from (at that time) selling computer OSs. So the Unix source code was distributed relatively freely to universities (it cost $1.00 for a university to lease the OS). As a result, Unix gained favor within the academic/research community and formed the basis for Operating Systems instructions in the leading universities. Graduating students took their knowledge with them into the business community where many applications were written for the many variations of the original Unix OS (Linux, AIX, Solaris, HPUX, Berkley Unix, Xenix, etc.). It was familiarity with Unix that prompted Linus Torvalds to write Linux (because he was unsatisfied with Microsoft's DOS) and freely release it to anyone who wanted to use it[21], thereby starting the **open source** movement.

## Single user Operating Systems

A single user OS is intended for one computer to be used by one person at a time. Early OSs could only have one profile, but OSs such as Windows XP allowed multiple people to use the same system at different times by having each person log in, which created multiple profiles that stored configuration information for each user.

One popular microcomputer that has a proprietary OS is the Macintosh, which has set it apart from all the other microcomputers. The Macintosh computer OS grew out of the Lisa, the first commercially sold microcomputer with a *graphical user interface*. A graphical user interface uses pictures called icons and menus clicked on with a mouse instead of commands typed into the system on a command line (called a *command line interface*). (See the story of the graphical user interface.)

Until Microsoft released the very first OS (Microsoft Disk Operating System, or MSDOS), most OSs were designed and sold specifically for one type of hardware. MSDOS, however, could be installed on any machine that was *IBM-compatible* (so named

**The Story of the GUI**

Many people believe that Steve Jobs from Apple computer designed the interface that we now know as Graphical User Interface (GUI), but he did not. Instead, Jobs was convinced by some of his employees to visit Xerox labs in 1979, where he saw the Alto computer. The Alto was different than all the other computers of the day; it used a mouse and menus or icons (little pictures) instead of a keyboard to enter most commands. It also displayed windows on the screen, and had a trash can in which the user could "drop" files they wanted to delete.

Steve Jobs liked what he saw, and he made a deal with Xerox so that the researchers could work with Apple to develop the Lisa computer (named after Steve Job's daughter, although ostensibly it was an acronym for Local Integrated Software Architecture). The Apple Lisa did not sell well because it was expensive, slow, and beset with unreliable hardware, but it formed the foundation for both the Macintosh computer and the Windows GUI interface.

In 1988 Apple sued Microsoft for infringing on the "look and feel" of the GUI, but lost in court at the end of a four year battle because they had earlier licensed the technology to Microsoft for Windows 1.0. In the meantime, Xerox sued Apple since they were actually the originator of the look and feel of the GUI. Their suit was never pressed, however, because the statute of limitations had run out.

---

[21] The story of the beginning of Linux can be found at http://www.bellevuelinux.org/linus.html, written by the Linux Information Project, last updated January 24, 2006 and accessed May, 2008.

because IBM leased the DOS software from Microsoft for the first microcomputer, the IBM-PC in August of 1981). Buying hardware from one vendor and software from another was the next phase of the 1969 anti-trust legislation which forced IBM to unbundle hardware purchases from software purchases. However, DOS had a command line interface, so Microsoft went on to develop Windows, the much easier-to-use interface that would work with many different hardware systems.

The advantage of a command line interface is power , speed, and flexibility. If you already know the commands, it is much faster to type them into the computer than to use a mouse to click on the limited choices. Additionally, (again, if you already know the commands) there are hundreds of thousands of commands and their options that will allow you to do exactly what you need to do. For example, in Figure 7, the DOS commands are written to create a new folder, open the folder, and list everything that is in the folder. (You can get to the DOS prompt by either choosing *DOS Prompt* from the Accessory menu or choosing *Run* from the Start button and typing *cmd* into the dialog box.)

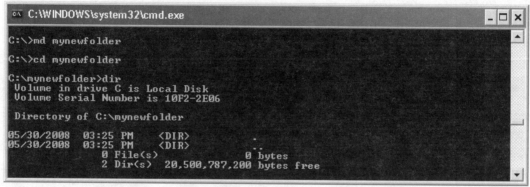

**Figure 7  Command Line Interface (DOS)**

Obviously, if you already know the commands, a command line interface is faster, more flexible, and more powerful. There, however, is the rub. Very few people already know the commands. The main advantage of the GUI is that you don't have to memorize the commands. It is much easier to use, and therefore accessible to many more people than esoteric and difficult-to-remember computer commands.

While the GUI aspect of Windows was one reason for its popularity, there was another underlying reason for the astronomical growth of Windows. Prior to Windows, every program that people purchased and installed on their computer had a different way of doing things. For example, to save in Wordperfect (the #1 wordprocessor at the time) you pressed the F10 key. To save in Lotus 123 (the #1 spreadsheet at the time) you pressed /FS (slash, F for File, S for Save). Every time you purchased a new program, you had to learn, from scratch, which keys did which things. Additionally, each program required you to install "drivers" (instructional files for peripherals such as printers and monitors and keyboards). You had to get the driver from the manufacturer of the peripheral. For example, if you had purchased an HP Laserjet printer, you would receive a floppy disk (remember, there was no Internet at this time). Following the instructions in the WordPerfect manual, you would install the printer using the floppy disk from HP. Then you had to follow the instructions in the Lotus 123 manual to install the printer for that program as well, which used a completely different method of printing to the printer. Additionally, if you had an enhanced keyboard (the kind with a number pad on the side), you had to go through the same rigamarole for the keyboard. And for the monitor. And for the mouse. And so on.

Windows eliminated many of these headaches by standardizing the way programs interfaced with peripherals. Instead of printing directly to the printer, the application would use the Windows interface to handle the printer driver. Each printer, therefore, only had to be installed once for all applications instead of for each application individually. This capability led to the *plug and play* feature discussed in the first chapter in the 640k barrier section.

Additionally, Windows standardized the way programs did simple actions like opening and saving files. All Windows-compatible programs opens a file by going to the File menu and clicking the Open choice. All Windows-compatible programs saves a file by going to the File menu and clicking the Save choice.

Because applications rely upon the Windows interface to handle basic commands, the lifecycle of an OS is very influential in the entire industry. Although some applications can run on different OSs (usually by running an emulator program that mimics the environment of the earlier OS), most of the time when you upgrade OSs you must purchase new applications. Furthermore, because the OS handles commands directly to the hardware, newer OSs often demand newer hardware. While it was possible, for example, to "upgrade" a Windows 95 machine to Windows 98 without too much trouble, the major hardware advances built into Windows XP meant that it was virtually impossible to "upgrade". To run Windows XP you had to purchase a new computer. (The same is true for Vista - it is difficult to upgrade an XP machine to Vista.) When an OS is no longer being supported, that means that applications will no longer be written for it, and fixes for new problems will not become available. The release and support cycles of Windows OSs can be seen in Figure 8.

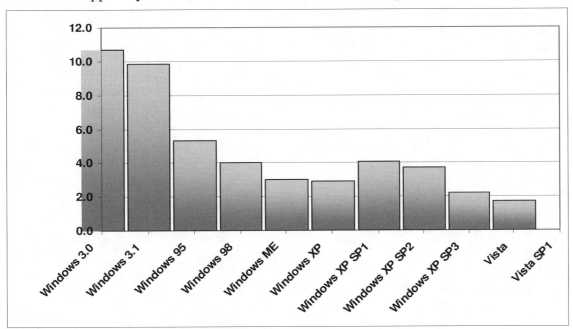

**Figure 8 The shrinking lifecycle of operating systems**

Because of the application's and hardware's reliance on the OS, people purchasing computers are best off buying them in "generations", trying to, as much as possible, purchase the hardware, OS, and application software that are all at peak popularity about the same time.

---

### When is the best time to buy a computer?

The best time to purchase a microcomputer is about 2 years after the release of a new OS. Earlier than that, and the hardware manufacturers and application publishers have not had enough time to upgrade their components for the OS. Later than that and many manufacturers or applications publishers are already focused on making changes necessary for the next version of the OS.

Furthermore, it makes sense to hold off on any "patches" or "upgrades" until they've been fully tested. Microsoft has instituted an automatic updating feature in its new OSs, but it is usually best to set it to let you know when there are updates, but not to do the update for a few weeks. That way, other people's system will find the bugs in the system and Microsoft will fix them before you even download the update.

---

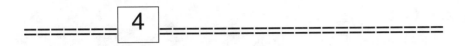

# Chapter 4: Hardware and Peripherals

Underneath the OS is the hardware. All computers (mainframes, servers, and microcomputers) all contain the same basic components although they are often called different things. Because most people only come into contact with the microcomputer, we will focus on that type of hardware in this chapter.

## Why You Need To Know Hardware

Imagine that you went to your car mechanic and told them that you couldn't turn the steering wheel. They spend 3 hours working on your steering only to find out that your tires are flat. Who would be the "dumb" one - you for telling them something was wrong with your steering wheel, or them for not noticing that the tires were all flat? In the world of automobiles, this would never happen. Even though you are just a driver, not a mechanic, you know how to recognize when a tire is flat. You understand what part the tires play in allowing you to turn the steering wheel so that you can drive around.

But imagine a world where this is not the case. Where some mechanics only look at steering wheels and have no responsibility whatsoever for the tires - so much so that they wouldn't even look at them. In this world, you would have to know the parts yourself. You would have to know how to figure out which type of mechanic to go to - the one who deals with the steering wheel or the one who deals with the tires.

Because in the world of computers there are different technologies for the different parts, no one technician can diagnose problems for different technologies. Furthermore, this makes is especially difficult to diagnose issues between the different parts. Therefore, an end user must be able to recognize the different components and what type of support they might need when there are problems. You will need knowledge of basic components in order to communicate with technology professionals trying to figure out what's wrong with your machine.

The technology map introduced in the first chapter is very helpful here. The first question to figure out is whether or not the problem is with the network, the hardware or the software. It would do no good to take your computer to a computer repair shop if the problem is that your network connection doesn't work. Complaining to the publisher of a new program you purchased to publish DVDs will do no good if your DVD drive on your computer doesn't work. It is your responsibility to identify which general area has the problem in order to identify the proper person to fix it.

# The Basic Hardware Components

A typical microcomputer is shown in Figure 9. Look at the picture of the inside of a computer in Figure 10. Inside a computer will be:

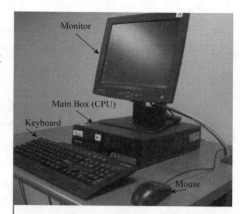

**Figure 9 Basic Microcomputer System**

♦ A motherboard – the main integrated circuit board that connects everything together, usually made of green plastic with many other items connected either by solder or clipped on.

♦ A power supply – to provide power.

♦ A cooling fan – because computer chips stop working reliably when they get hot, (and sometimes they get very hot). There may also be a "heat sink" which is designed to absorb the heat and keep it away from the chips.

♦ ROM chip – Read Only Memory chip – usually containing the beginning instructions to the computer that it reads when it is turned on. ROM chips are actually firmware, a combination of software and hardware.

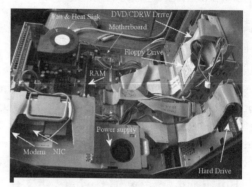

**Figure 10  Inside a Microcomputer**

♦ RAM chip – Random Access Memory chip – empty storage for information that is only available when the computer is on. RAM can usually be added to the motherboard in order to improve performance. (See Figure 11)

♦ CPU – Central Processing Unit chip – the thinking part of the computer (ie – the brain). (See Figure 11)

**Figure 11 Close-ups of RAM, CPU, Internal Battery & Hard drive**

♦ A hard drive – (ie – the C: Drive) to store all the software and all the data.  Also called a hard disk or a Winchester disk.

♦ A CD-ROM or a CD-RW drive - to transfer large amounts of data from one computer to another.  CD-ROM stands for Compact Disc, Read Only Media and CD-RW stands for Compact Disc, Read-Write.

♦ A DVD player or DVD writer.  Digital Video Disc - a newer type of media that can store more data than a CD.  DVD is not just the media - it refers to the format that enables the DVD to present menus and play video.

♦ A speaker – so you can hear sounds and music.
♦ Video Card – a card that makes your video monitor look better or work faster (especially if you want to play high quality video games).

**Figure 12 Connections and Ports**

♦ Modem – a card that allows your computer to connect to the public telephone system. (See Figure 12.)
♦ Network Interface Card (NIC)– a card that allows your computer to connect to other computers or devices. Most NICs these days are Ethernet 10/100. (See Figure 12.)
♦ USB Interface - Universal Serial Bus - a newer type of connector that is more universal than either parallel or serial interfaces. Most printers, external hard drives, cameras, flash memory and other peripheral devices use USB connections. (See Figure 12.)
♦ Firewire Interface - a type of connection that is newer than parallel and serial, but older than USB. It was originally designed to handle the high speed transmission needs of video and voice.
♦ Parallel Interface – an older type of connector usually used for the printer (and sometimes other devices). (See Figure 12.)
♦ Serial Interface – an older type of connector used for various devices like external modems and cameras. (See Figure 12.)
♦ A floppy drive – to transfer small amounts of data from one computer to another (though fewer and fewer computers have floppy drives anymore).
♦ Video Interface – a connector for the monitor. Sometimes this connector is on the video card instead of directly on the motherboard. (See Figure 12.)

Even though there is a specific chip called the CPU, sometimes people call the entire box the "CPU". Anything that is inside the main box (also referred to as a desktop, or a tower, or a workstation) is considered internal to the computer. As noted earlier, different types of computers may have any of these components in the main box (though they are often called something different. For example, a hard drive in a mainframe is called DASD (pronounced Dazzdy), which stands for Direct Access Storage Device. Anything outside the computer is considered a peripheral (discussed later in the chapter).

# Types of Computers

Mainframe have a few brands, models, and types. IBM started the field in the sixties, and is still one of the top mainframe and manufacturers. They started with the 700 series, increased their dominance with the 360 series, and retain the top spot with the zSeries, which was developed as a partnership with Hitachi, a Japanese manufacturer. Unisys is the only other manufacturers left in the United States. Hitachi, Fujistu, Oki and NEC are all in Japan, while Siemens and Telefunken hail from Germany. While most mainframe computers these days are designed to work with PCs connected to them, they also still work with terminals.

> **The Mainframe Industry Story**
>
> In the early seventies, the mainframe market was very competitive, although IBM always had the lion's share of the market. At the time, there were often references to *IBM and the Seven Dwarfs*, referring to Burroughs, UNIVAC, NCR, Control Data, Honeywell, General Electric and RCA. Later, as the market began shrinking, the phrase changed to *IBM and the BUNCH*, referring to Burroughs, UNIVAC, NCR, Control Data, and Honeywell. Today, the only survivor as a mainframe manufacturers is IBM. The remnants of General Electric, RCA, UNIVAC and Burroughs can be found in Unisys. Honeywell was bought out by Groupe Bull, and NCR was bought out by AT&T before being spun off again in 1996. At that point, NCR refocused on its core business; point-of-sale devices (cash registers, now combined with bar code scanners).

There is another category called the supercomputer, which is generally associated with Cray (known as the supercomputer company, though its founder, Seymour Cray never used the term supercomputer). A supercomputer differs from a mainframe computer in that it is generally a one-of-a-kind system devoted to a single program, such as forecasting the weather, or doing intense calculations for research or graphics animation.

Another category that has fallen by the wayside is minicomputer. In the early days of computers, the minicomputer category referred to those systems not large enough to be mainframes, but too big to be considered microcomputers. With the exception of IBM, all the vendors of minicomputers have been acquired or closed: Digital Equipment Corporation (DEC), Data General, Prime Computer and Wang. IBM now uses the phrase "midrange systems" to refer to their iSeries (formerly known as the AS/400, the epitome of a minicomputer). The minicomputer term has largely been supplanted by the use of Unix-type OSs which are generally considered to run on servers or workstations rather than minicomputers. HP and Sun both refer to their systems as servers rather than minicomputers.

The term microcomputer is still in use, but not used as often as a variety of other terms that may refer to the same thing; personal computer (PC), desktop, tower, laptop, notebook, or just computer. The term PC usually refers to all personal computers, including those manufactured by Apple computer which uses the Macintosh OS, but sometimes is used to differentiate computers from a variety of manufacturers who install the Windows OS from the Macintosh systems. In other words, sometimes PC includes Macs, and sometimes it only means Windows-based machines.

The term desktop is often used to refer to a microcomputer because often the computer sits on top of a desk. Sometimes this term means all personal computers, and other times it is used to differentiate the microcomputer from computers that are in data centers, such as servers. It can also be used to distinguish desktop computers from those that are mobile, as in laptop or notebook computers. (Although notebook computers were originally smaller than laptop computers, the difference has largely disappeared as laptop computers have become extremely small. Macintosh recently released the MacBook Air, which is small enough to fit into a typical manila envelop. See Figure 13.)

The term tower came into use because sometimes computers sit wide and flat (as in desktop), and sometimes they sit narrow and tall (as in tower). However, some people use the term *tower* to refer to the CPU, the main box of the personal computer as opposed to the peripherals.

Personal digital assistants (PDAs) are also powerful enough to be considered computing devices, although they are also considered peripherals. The first commercially produced PDA was the Apple Newton in 1992. The Apple Newton was not a commercial success, but introduced important innovations such as the touch screen, stroke recognition, synchronizing with a calendar and desktop

> **Server as hardware or software**
>
> The term *server* can be very confusing because it is used in two completely different contexts. When talking about hardware, server means a more powerful computer than a PC, one designed to have many different PCs connected to it. It is a physical box designed to serve something (usually files or applications) connected to a network.
>
> However, when talking about software, the term server is also used. But in this case, server is referring to an application running on the system. These server applications are not limited to physical servers, nor are they limited to one per system. A physical server might be running an application server, a web server, a fax server, a print server, and a mail server all at the same time. But so can a mainframe computer, or even a desktop computer. If I have three computers in my home, but only one of them is connected to a printer, when I print to that printer *through* the connected PC, it is acting as a print server.
>
> It is generally this software server that we refer to when we discuss *client server* architecture. Client server is concept that a piece of software (client) running on one machine (usually a desktop) works in tandem with a piece of software (called a server) running on another machine (also called a server). For example, when you look at a web page, your client software (Internet Explorer or Firefox) interacts with the web server (Apache or IIS).

**Figure 13 MacBook Air - the thinnest laptop anywhere.**

applications such as wordprocessing and spreadsheets. The next commercially produced PDA was the Palm Pilot followed by many others including the Handspring Visor and its successor, the popular Treo. (In 2003 Palm bought Handspring, and in 2005 Palm was bought by Robotics, Inc.)

In January of 1999 the PDA industry was rocked by the introduction of a new device from Research In Motion (RIM), a Canadian company. RIM unveiled the Blackberry, a device that included a miniature keyboard instead of the touch screen. Furthermore, instead of just synchronizing with a PC, the Blackberry could send and receive email *from anywhere.* Using wireless connection technology, the Blackberry wirelessly downloaded email continuously so that busy executives were never out of touch. In March of 2002 the Blackberry 5810 was released, the first Blackberry to include phone capabilities. RIM became the first company to combine the cell phone and a PDA in the same device.

Since then, cell phone technology has been getting smarter and smarter as RIM has leased its email capability to many phone manufacturers, which required them to add keyboards to the cell phone devices. Cell phones also started to include built-in digital cameras (both video and still picture). Furthermore, some phones are now beginning to include Global Positioning Systems (GPS), which can provide step by step directions to help people navigate. The iPhone, a new device from Apple, combines the capability of a cell phone with the music fidelity of an iPod. (IPod is a portable media player released in 2001 coupled with iTunes, a jukebox application that allows people to quickly and easily purchase, download, and manage the music on their iPod.)

> **Smart Phones and their Ease of Use**
> You know that telephones have become smarter because they are no longer easy to use. Even technical people have difficulty. Bjarne Stroustrup, designer of the C++ computer programming language famously said; "*I have always wished for my computer to be as easy to use as my telephone; my wish has come true because I can no longer figure out how to use my telephone.*"

It is only a matter of time before all of these capabilities converge. New cell phones will include keyboards, the ability to search the World Wide Web, the ability to send and receive email, cameras, GPS applications, jukeboxes, calendars, wordprocessing, spreadsheets, and the ability to synchronize with more powerful computing devices.

As cell phones become smarter, so do computers become more powerful. One of the most important things for a business person to know is how powerful their computer is. The next section will talk about the three indicators of computing power: memory, storage, and CPU.

## Power: Processor, Memory and Storage

A computer has three attributes which identifies it's *power*. The first is the speed and volume capability in the central processing unit (CPU). The second is the amount of space in the random access memory (RAM). The third is the amount of space in the hard drive (HD) to store applications and data.

When you buy a computer, or talk to others about a computer, you should have a basic idea of how powerful the computer is. You should know how much hard drive space you have, how fast your processor is, and how much memory you have. In order to understand all the different measurements, however, we need to discuss bits, bytes, k, megs, and gigs.

## *Bits, Bytes, K, Megs, and Gigs*

There is nothing more confusing than the terminology and usage for measuring technology concepts such as memory, hard drive space, and data transfer speeds. The confusion comes from the fact that sometimes these items are measured in binary measurements (such as k byte), and sometimes they are measured in decimal measurements (such as kilobyte). The difference between a K byte and a kilobyte are often ignored (until you try to figure out why the numbers never add up).

Furthermore, common usage of terms is different depending upon the industry. The telecom industry typically measures data speeds in decimal kilobits per second (kbit/s) or megabits per second (Mbit/s). The hard drive industry measures hard drive space in decimal megabytes or decimal gigabytes, which translates into a smaller number of binary megabytes or gigabytes. For example A 100 decimal gigabyte hard drive, (100GB HD), only has 93.1 binary gigabytes (or 97,656,250 bytes). The memory industry, on the other hand, measures in binary K bytes. 1 gigabyte of memory (1GiB RAM), therefore, is equivalents to 1,048,576,000 bytes.

A bit (**b**inary dig**it**) is always a bit, and a byte is always a byte. Both are the same whether being measured in decimal or binary notation, and 8 bits always equals one byte. In decimal notation, however, there are 1000 bits in a kilobit, 1000 kilobits in a megabit, 1000 megabits in a gigabit, 1000 gigabits in a terabit. Additionally, there are 1000 bytes in a kilobyte, 1000 kilobytes in a megabyte, and 1000 megabytes in a gigabyte.

In binary notation, on the other hand, there are 1024 bytes in a K byte, and 1024 K bytes in a megabyte, 1024 megabytes in a gigabyte, and 1024 gigabytes in a terabyte, 1024 terabytes in a petabyte and 1024 petabytes in a exabyte. (There are also 1024 bits in a K bit, 1024 K bits in a megabit, and 1024 megabits in a gigabit).

Unfortunately, many people refer to these measurements with a shortened name: K, meg, and gig - without specifying whether or not they are talking bits or bytes, or binary or decimal. For technical folk, that's not a problem because they understand from the context which one was meant. If you are dealing with memory, meg refers to megabytes using the k byte conversion (binary). If you are dealing with hard drive space, meg refers to megabytes using the kilobyte conversion (decimal). If you were dealing with data speed, meg refers to megabits per second (decimal). Most people are not technical enough to understand the nuanced differences, however, so most just accept whatever nomenclature they are given by the vendors and don't bother trying to convert between the different measurements.

In the earliest days of the computers it was easy to tell the difference between memory and storage because storage (the hard drive) was usually in Megs and memory (RAM) was usually in K. In 1985 the IBM PC would traditionally come with **128 K bytes** of memory and a **10 Megabyte** hard drive. These days, that's not even enough memory for your cell phone!

Now that both memory and storage are often measured in megabytes and gigabytes, there is more confusion than ever. In an effort to decrease the confusion, a new nomenclature has been proposed (but which is not yet in common usage. Nonetheless, to avoid confusion the new nomenclature will be used throughout the rest of this book) The International Electro-technical Commission (IEC) adopted the standard nomenclature shown to more clearly clarify if the measurement used refers to bit or byte, binary or decimal, as shown in Table 4.

**Table 4  IEC standards for binary measurements of memory and storage.**

| Full technical name | Proposed Prefix | Proposed Symbol | Numeric Multiplier | # of binary Bytes |
|---|---|---|---|---|
| kilobinary | kibi- | Ki | $2^{10}$ | 1,024 |
| megabinary | mebi- | Mi | $2^{20}$ | 1,048,576 |
| gigabinary | gibi- | Gi | $2^{30}$ | 1,073,741,824 |
| terabinary | tebi- | Ti | $2^{40}$ | 1,099,511,627,776 |
| petabinary | pebi- | Pi | $2^{50}$ | 1,125,899,906,842,620 |
| exabinary | exbi- | Ei | $2^{60}$ | 1,152,921,504,606,850,000 |

If adopted into common usage, the terminology shown in Table 5 would be used.

**Table 5  Terms and their abbreviations for IEC standard.**

| Term | Abbreviation | Reference measurement |
|---|---|---|
| bit | bit | 0 or 1 |
| byte | B | 8 bits |
| kibibit | Kibit | 1024 bits |
| kilobit | kbit | 1000 bits |
| kibibyte (binary) | KiB | 1024 bytes |
| kilobyte (decimal) | kB | 1000 bytes |
| megabit | Mbit | 1000 kilobits |
| mebibyte (binary) | MiB | 1024 kibibytes |
| megabyte (decimal) | MB | 1000 kilobytes |
| gigabit | Gbit | 1000 megabits |
| gibibyte (binary) | GiB | 1024 mebibytes |
| gigabyte (decimal) | GB | 1000 megabytes |

| Term | Abbreviation | Reference measurement |
|------|--------------|----------------------|
| terabit | Tbit | 1000 gigabits |
| tebibyte (binary) | TiB | 1024 gibibytes |
| terabyte (decimal) | TB | 1000 gigabytes |
| petabit | Pbit | 1000 terabits |
| pebibyte (binary) | PiB | 1024 tebibytes |
| petabyte (decimal) | PB | 1000 terabytes |
| exabit | Ebit | 1000 petabits |
| exbibyte (binary) | EiB | 1024 pebibytes |
| exabyte (decimal) | EB | 1000 petabytes |

Now that we have discussed the differences between bits, bytes, megs, and gigs, we can move on to understanding the three different aspects of computing power; the processor, the memory, and the hard drive space.

## *The Processor*

If you have a PC (personal computer based on the original IBM personal computer model) you probably have a Pentium central processing chip (CPU) from Intel or an Athlon from AMD inside it. If you have a Macintosh, you probably have a G3 or G4 chip from Motorola (although Apple has switched to Intel chips in the last few years). Although there are only a few chip vendors, there are hundreds of varieties of CPU chips and intense competition for new computer models.

Another aspect of a CPU is the Clock Speed. Clock speed has nothing to do with the time. It is a measurement of how fast your CPU can process instructions, but keep in mind that clock speed is only distantly related to how fast your computer is. A low clock speed is a limiting factor – if your application is ready to roll, but it has to wait for the next "internal pulse" it could be slowed down a little. But we are talking nanoseconds – much too small a time frame for a human being to notice any delay. The truth is the application is rarely waiting for the internal pulse. Most of the time when you experience a delay it is because the application is waiting for the hard drive, the monitor, or the network; all perceptibly slower than the CPU. The memory, hard drive, monitor, and/or network will affect your computer's speed much more than clock speed. (Remember that the next time your neighbor brags about their 2 Gigagahertz clock speed – it really doesn't matter!)

You might hear about a Dual-Core Pentium or Athlon chip, which means that instead of just one processor in the chip, there are two. The processors share the load (but also need to be coordinated, which is called "overhead", so you actually get less than two times the performance).

The next big leap is the Itanium chip which is based on 64-bit architecture. (The Pentium chip is based upon 32-bit architecture.) Itanium chips are usually only used in high-end servers. Applications written for 32 bit computing don't work on 64 bit machines, and visa versa, so an end user would have major difficulty finding applications that run on an Itanium chip.

## *Memory*

Memory is the "working space" your computer uses for immediate processing. Memory is *volatile* which means that when you turn your computer off, everything in memory disappears. If you are writing a letter in a wordprocessor and haven't yet saved it to disk, for example, then it is only in memory. If someone were to trip over the power cord of your computer, you would lose the letter you are working on and would have to retype it.

Too little memory is often the cause of slow computers. More memory means that the processor doesn't have to dip into the hard drive as often to pick up information. Hard drives are much slower (even at 300 revolutions per second) than integrated circuit chips (which go at the speed of conduction – effectively as fast as the speed of light). (In some textbooks, you will see hard drives referred to as "secondary memory", but that terminology is rarely used among today's information technology staff.)

The amount of memory you should install is based upon the needs of the OS. The amount of memory needed by various selected OSs is shown in Table 6. The requirements have all been converted into Megabytes (binary) so that they can more easily be compared.

**Table 6 Table of operating systems with RAM requirements**

| Operating System | Recommended minimum RAM |
|---|---|
| Windows 98 | 24 Mebibytes |
| Windows 2000 Server | 64 Mebibytes |
| Windows XP | 128 Mebibytes |
| Solaris | 512 Mebibytes |
| Macintosh Leopard | 512 Mebibytes |
| Linux | 512 Mebibytes |
| Windows Vista | 1024 Mebibytes |
| Windows 2008 Server | 2048 Mebibytes |

## *Hard Drive*

The other determiner of power of your computer is the amount of space on your hard drive. These days, a typical PC will come with 80 to 180 Gigabytes (decimal) of hard drive space. Only five years ago, the typical hard drive was 20 or 40 Gigabytes. (And remember, in 1985, a typical hard drive was **10 megabytes.**)

One reason for the dramatic increase in hard drive space is the space requirements of the OS. In 1985 the operating system was DOS, and it took up less than 2 megabytes of space. In 1998 a typical hard drive was 100 Megabytes, and the Windows 98 OS took up about 20 MB. Of the 89 Gigabyte hard drive of today, the Windows Vista OS will take up 10 GB. Furthermore, a portion of your hard drive is used dynamically by Windows for virtual memory, and that can use up space as well. (If you are ever looking at the root of your hard drive and notice a huge file called hiberfil.sys that you cannot delete, that is where Windows is storing the virtual memory).

Another reason for the larger hard drives is that people nowadays need space for graphics, music, and video. Plain text files are tiny. You can fit the whole library of congress on a couple of CDs if you leave out the pictures. At the same time, a single photo uses up over one megabyte. One minute of video uses up 10 Megs of your hard drive. A full length 90 minute movie uses a Gig. You can pretty quickly use up your hard drive if you download photos and videos frequently.

The practical aspect of understanding the general size of different types of files is in knowing how much space you need to store information. In Table 7 you can see how much space typical files might take up on a hard drive or other storage medium. Notice that the chart gives you both the accurate assessment of the names and amounts and relationships for the terms, as well as an "about a" references that can help gauge how big or small something is. "About a" compares the size of the item to the storage medium that would hold the item.

## Hardware Peripherals

Peripherals are devices attached to the main computer. They may include:

- Printer
- Keyboard
- Mouse
- Monitor
- Speakers
- Digital Camera
- Digital Video Camera
- Cell phone
- Scanner
- PDA (personal digital assistant, like a Blackberry)
- Modem
- Cable Modem
- Router
- DSL switch (Digital Subscriber Line)
- Tape Drive
- Hard Drive
- Projector
- Rollerball
- CD-WR drive
- DVD drive
- Flash drive (also known as a key drive, thumb drive, or memory stick

Peripherals can be categorized as either *input* devices or *output* devices. An input device enables people or other devices to enter information into a computer. An output device enables a person or other device to receive information from a computer. A mouse, keyboard, camera, and scanner are input devices. A monitor, printer, and projector are all output devices. Some devices can perform as either input or output, such as flash drives, hard drives, or networking devices such as routers or DSL switches.

**Table 7  Amount of space needed for typical files**

| What? | How big?[22] | Related to … | About a. .. |
|---|---|---|---|
| Single page of text only | 2 KB | 2/1000$^{th}$ of a meg, | You can fit 375,000,000 of them on a compact disc. |
| Single 8 color graphic picture | 500 KB | ½ of a meg | You can fit 1500 of them on a compact disc. |
| Single Word document ten pages with graphics | 1 MB | 1 Meg | You can fit 750,000 of them on a compact disc. |
| Full color photo | 2 MB | 2 times the size of a meg | You can fit 375 of them on a compact disc. |
| A 3 minute 2X3 inch video | 10 MB | 10 times the size of a gig | Can fit on a compact disc. |
| A 5 minute full screen video | 150 MB | 150 times the size of a gig | Can fit 3 on a compact disc (but will not play on a DVD player) |
| A database of thousands of records | 200 MB | 200 times the size of a meg | You can fit 3 of them on a compact disc. |
| A Powerpoint presentation (with graphics, photos, and animations) | 500 MB | Half a gig | Can fit 1 on a compact disc |
| A full screen full length video (movie) | 1 GB | 1 Gig | Cannot fit on compact disc - must use digital video disc (DVD) |
| A databases with millions of records | 2 GB | Twice the size of a gig | Cannot fit on a compact disc; use a flash drive or digital video disc. |
| An accounting system for a Fortune 1000 company (for a couple of years) | 250 GB | 250 times the size of a gig | RAID Hard drive system on server (too big for PC) |
| Datamart | 500 GB | Half a Terabyte | External storage - usually a series of hard drives |
| Datawarehouse | 10 TB | 10 times the size of a Terabyte | External storage - usually an array of hard drives. |

---

[22] Keep in mind that none of these sizes is meant to be exact as the actual size of files varies wildly. But the sizes will give you an understanding of the *relative* size for each type of file.

# Chapter 5: World Wide Web & Other Internet Applications

Now that we have covered hardware and software, we can begin to talk about some of the applications and devices related to how businesses and people connect to each other using the world wide web and the Internet.

## The Difference between WWW and Internet

The public Internet is a worldwide internetwork of computers and computer networks. It was developed through the efforts of hundreds of people, but primarily Bob Kahn at Bolt Beranek and Newman (a consulting firm) and Vint Cerf at Stanford University. (See the inset for the story of the Internet.).

Shortly after the Internet came about, Timothy Berners-Lee and Robert Cailliau developed an easy-to-use interface (a system of hyperlinks) that sat on top of the public Internet. The system of hyperlinking is called the World Wide Web. A hyperlink is an object (a picture or word) that is programmed so that if you click on it with a mouse, you will jump to a new location to view a new page. Suddenly, someone with no technical training at all could connect to any other computer on the public Internet network, and could retrieve information from any of those computers. (To be accurate, it felt like suddenly, but actually it took many years. The Internet started functioning in 1982, and the World Wide Web was invented in 1990.)

Many people use the terms World Wide Web and Internet interchangeably, but the truth is they are two completely different things. The World Wide Web is an application (a giant shared application, but an application nonetheless) that runs on *top of* the Internet, no different than email or search engines. Because of the World Wide Web, all we have to do to connect to any computer anywhere in the world is click a mouse.

In keeping with our top-down approach to explaining the layers, we will focus on the applications that run on top of the Internet and how the Internet is utilized by businesses today first. Then the Internet protocols and devices are discussed in detail. The following chapter will delve into the details of the underlying physical network which forms the infrastructure of the Internet including the cabling and connection options.

### *The Story of the Internet*[23]

During the Cold War, the United States military became concerned with ensuring success in the event of a nuclear war. At that time, it was thought that the main deterrent against a Soviet nuclear attack was the threat of total nuclear retaliation by the Americans. During the late 1950s and early 1960s, in the midst of the Korean and Vietnam wars, a think tank project (paid for by the US Department of Defense and run by the RAND Corporation) led the way in nuclear strategic thinking. Paul Baran (who joined RAND Corporation in 1959) was particularly focused on finding a way to enhance the reliability of the communication links between offices of the United States military which were, in his mind, dangerously weak and fragile. At the time, the only type of data communication was point to point, which meant that an actual wire connected from one computer to another computer. If the single connection was broken (as it would be, undoubtedly, if a bomb were dropped on it), then no communication could take place. He was afraid that at a critical moment for nuclear retaliatory forces, point to point communication links would fail.

For years the think tank at RAND had been trying to invent a robust communications system - but with no success until Paul Baran joined the team. He came up with the three concepts that would give a communications system the robustness necessary to survive a nuclear bomb:
1. a distributed network instead of a centralized one.
2. massive amounts of redundancy built into the network.
3. breaking the message up into separate "packets", each of which would contain some of the file.

The thinking was that a distributed network could keep working, even after a lot of damage. If a message sender did not receive an acknowledgement of the message sent immediately, the sender would simply send it again and again until acknowledged or timed out. Additionally, a packet would also contain both the source and final address, and a sequence number to reassemble the packets in the right order once they all reached their destination.

It was these concepts that were used by Bob Kahn (at Bolt Beranek and Newman) and Vint Cerf (at Stanford University) when they were hired by the Department of Defense to develop a communication method to share research. They operationalized Paul Baran's ideas by developing Transmission Control Protocol/Internet Protocol (TCP/IP) which is the basis for all Internet connections.

In the early 1990s, the United States government handed over management of TCP/IP to a private company and opened it up to commercial venture, mainly due to the influence of Al Gore. (Many people fault Al Gore, thinking that he boasted imaginary credit for the public Internet, but the fact is that Al Gore helped create the public Internet by opening up the management so that it could be used by everyone, not just the government.[24])

# E-strategy

Businesses have been around for thousands of years and that the Internet has only been around for ten. Nonetheless, businesses have reacted speedily to the new capabilities that never existed before. The early years were very rocky (as described in the first chapter on the Dot Com Fever), but eventually most businesses find a way to develop a strategy for using the Internet, an "e-strategy" if you will.

---

[23] *Internet Genesis* (2003) by Karl Kruszelnicki at http://www.abc.net.au/science/k2/moments/s42478.htm, accessed on May 10, 2008. Internet survive nuclear war: Myth! By Darrell Burkey written on Aug 15 2002 http://www.anu.edu.au/mail-archives/link/link0208/0311.html accessed on May 10, 2008.

[24] Cerf, V., and B. Kahn. September 30, 2000. IP: Al Gore's support of the Internet. http://www.interesting-people.org/archives/interesting-people/200009/msg00052.html (accessed June 7, 2007).

P. K. Agarwal, the director of California's Department of Technology Services[25] has identified five stages of e-strategy for government entities: (1) Publish, (2) Interact, (3) Transact, (4) Integrate, and (5) Transform. Research consultant John Hagelian from Forrester Research has identified three: (1) Deconstruct, (2) Reinvent, and (3) Breakaway. Gartner Group, another research firm, has also identified three: (1) using the Web as a marketing channel, (2) creation of a virtual organization, and (3) E-commerce and on-line customer service. Jeff Duffell of IC Solutions proposed a simplified list: (1) Product Communication, (2) Simple Product Selling, and (3) Customized Product /Full Integration.

From the perception of a business person, these lists are either too academic or missing stages. In 2000 a more practical list of e-strategy phases was published. There are six phases:

- Corporate presence
- Product/service information
- E-commerce
- Advanced E-commerce
- Intranet and extranet
- Community

## Corporate Presence

A corporate web site is often known as the business card web site or a brochureware site. Some companies spend millions designing just the right look and feel of their sites; others get a high school kid to put their company logo on a welcome page and link another page with a list of their products and services. But in both cases the Web site contains static information about a company.

## Product Information

Once businesses master the brochureware site, depending upon the businesses, they may be ready to start providing detailed product information on their web sites. This is more complicated than you may think.

In order to put dynamic information about products on the Web a company must think about databases, middleware, links to inventory systems and full-service Web service companies. In the early days, in order to avoid the high cost of integrating their Web inventory with physical or in-store inventory, many businesses simply set up their Web sites as a completely different storefront with separate inventory.

It didn't work well.

---

[25] Sander, T., and P. Taylor. 2006. *Place matters: Geographically enabling government.* The Center for Digital Government. Folsom CA. Available at http://www.centerdigitalgov.com/story.php?id=100608 (accessed December 3, 2007)

Customers complained bitterly. They couldn't return something to the store that they had purchased on-line. They might buy something on the Web only to find out later that the item was actually out of stock (unknown at the time of the order because the Web only gets updated in the evening). They might want something that is out of stock on the Web, without knowing that they could have easily gotten it in-stock at a local store.

Customers have the view that the Web inventory should be a reflection of the actual, real-time inventory at every moment. But synchronizing inventory between a live store and a live Web site is a real challenge. Non-technologists often don't realize the difference between an inventory control system that works just fine when there are people somewhere along the chain and an inventory control system that works when there are no live thinking human beings in the process. (For an example of why this is so, see the inset *The Challenge of Integrating Web Inventory with Live Inventory*.)

None of these problems are insurmountable, but for some businesses they are an obstacle to E-commerce. Therefore, to get around this complexity, many smaller businesses place the product information on-line and then provide a toll free number for people to call to order them - utilizing the Internet capabilities without going to the added expense of changing their inventory system.

> **The Challenge of Integrating Web Inventory with Live Inventory**
>
> Any operational manager responsible for inventory control can describe the myriad of difficulties in keeping track of inventory. Let's discuss just a smattering of common problems, mostly surrounding the difficulty of granularity.
>
> Granularity refers to the level at which a unique item exists. Imagine that we own a mom-and-pop knickknack store. We sell decorative candles. We can order a skid of candles from any one of three different vendors. We take the skid and break it apart into three levels of inventory: cases, boxes, and individual candles. The candles come in either small or large, and either red, blue, green, or white. For a small knickknack store none of this is any problem. When we sell the items, we know that the individual small candles are $2 (regardless of color) and the individual large candles are $4. A box of 12 small candles is $20, and a box of large candles is $40, a case of small is $240, and so on. When we want to reorder, we just take a look at the inventory that is left. If all the red candles are gone, we put them on the sheet to reorder.
>
> This process is easy for a human, but for a blind and dumb computer system it is very difficult. It is very difficult to properly figure out what items are in stock, how much to sell each candle for, which vendor to purchase from, and which items need to be reordered. Most inventory systems in use today don't work at that level of granularity, choosing to ignore color, for example, when identifying the SKU (stock keeping unit), resulting in only 18 unique identifying numbers instead of 72. These systems rely upon a human being who can easily recognize which color needs to be ordered. Unfortunately, that wouldn't work in an on-line system because people (oddly enough) don't want to be surprised by what color candle they ordered. Some on-line systems get around this by adding an "attribute" field and expecting the buyer to type in the color, or choose the color from the list. This, then, gets into a huge programming issue because each product would need a different attribute list. This is just one example of the complexity involved when trying to provide an on-line purchasing experience.

capabilities without going to the added expense of changing their inventory system.

## E-Commerce

E-commerce occurs when people can order the products and services directly from a Web site. This typically involves putting a catalog of items on-line and providing screens for ordering and paying for the items.

Setting up E-commerce is a little more complex than it looks. One solution to eliminating the complexity is to simply place products and services on someone else's Web site like Amazon.com or eBay.com—both of which are like distributors for on-line vendors. For Amazon, the costs range from 6 percent to 15 percent plus per transaction charges (a few more bucks). For eBay, the costs range from 6 percent plus an insertion fee of up to $5. These charges are in addition to the normal 3 percent to 6 percent charges for a credit card or PayPal sale.

Paypal is Ebay's payment processing subsidiary. Customers can pay with a credit card using Paypal It is an alternative to paying for a merchant account (the right to take credit card transactions) because basically Paypal is acting as a pseudo--merchant account. A Paypal account allows a business to transfer the funds paid by the customers to their bank, (minus the transaction fee to Paypal, of course).

Paypal, of course, is only for on-line transactions. In order to to take credit cards in a storefront, a business still needs to get a regular merchant account. Having an off-line solution for credit cards is always cheaper than having an on-line solution because card-present fees are generally lower than card-not-present fees. Remember that in all cases the vendor is responsible for fraudulent transactions, so there are also various fee-based security authentication schemes you that can be added to the basic processing chain. Some merchant services are also resellers of on-line payment gateways such as Authorize.Net or PayPal's Payflow (the back-end authorization gateway for PayPal merchant accounts), so it is possible to get both the on-line and the off-line accounts from the same merchant service.

The next consideration, of course, is the financial software being used. Most of the time, newer financial software provides a link between the accounting software and the merchant account and payment gateway. Of course, the oldest financial packages didn't link anywhere, and a business had to enter deposits and checks manually. It is not uncommon for organizations to still be doing it that way.

Now, however, the vendors of most financial software packages have made a deal with one or more merchant accounts and one or more payment gateways. Intuit, the owner of QuickBooks, for example, purchased Innovative Process Solutions a number of years ago, so they host their own payment gateway that is connected directly to the more recent versions of QuickBooks. QuickBooks, therefore, can be the vendor of the financial software, the merchant account, and the authorization gateway (for setup, monthly, and per-transaction fees, of course). QuickBooks also works with PayPal's Payflow and Authorize.net gateways as well.

## *Advanced E-Commerce*

There's E-commerce, and then there's **E-commerce**. After the first few attempts at putting products and services on-line, most companies realize that it is harder than it looks to get right. It's not just the look and feel of the screens that's important, it's the usability of the site. How easy is it to order? How quickly does the screen download? Does the site remember what customers ordered before, or do they have to enter their name and address every time they get on? Can they configure complex items when they order them? How easily can they find what they want? Can others comment on the quality of each of the products or services? Companies usually spend a great deal of time and effort in improving the usability of their Web sites.

### Intranet and Extranet

An intranet is when a company uses Internet technologies (such as TCP/IP, HTML[26], and Web sites) to provide their employees with access to needed information. For example, if a company puts absence request forms on a Web site for employees to download and fill out when they want a day off, they are implementing an intranet.

An extranet is using public Internet hardware, software, and protocols for making resources available to partners (such as vendors and representatives) outside of the internal network. The actual hardware and software is the same as an intranet.

To some extent, an extranet is used every time an employee emails someone outside of the company. But some companies have not yet embraced exchanging information electronically because of the inherent security issues with email. This is where an extranet can be very useful. By providing passwords and a secure encryption protocol (provided by most Web hosting services) and an encryption transfer method (often called a VPN or virtual private network), we can allow select people to use the public Internet to access private data that stays private.

The productive uses are infinite: allowing employees to work from home, providing literature to representatives, delivering promotional material to resellers, share project milestones with partners, share inventory needs with vendors, conduct on-line focus groups about products and services, and so on.

Both intranets and extranets are more complex than typical Web pages, so they require the use of a full-service hosting service or an internal team of IT support people or both. But the value can be tremendous.

### Community

One step further than an extranet is a real virtual community. For an on-line community, there must be a two-way dynamic purpose. A community is made up of people who associate with each other on the Web. The people in the community develop a relationship that is only peripherally related to the products and services they buy within the virtual walls of the community. They converse with each other (i.e., chat, email, and post), know each other, trust each other, and generally provide for each other's needs.

According to those in the industry, on-line communities are becoming the new strategic business mandate. They cite statistics about how many millions of people are members of popular on-line communities such as Facebook (for youth) and LinkedIn (for business professionals). MySpace.com, a popular on-line community, was started by a band that wanted more fans to come hear them play, but soon it became a hot spot for teens to hang out.

---

[26] HTML stands for HyperText Markup Language, which is covered in more detail later in the chapter, as is TCP/IP (Transmission Control Protocol, Internet Protocol).

Some products have become successful due entirely to the virtual buzz surrounding them created by vendor-supported communities. One of the earliest on-line community marketing success stories was the Big Green Egg, (Figure 14) which is a high-priced ceramic grill. Devoted fans post frequently on www.biggreenegg.com and that attracts others who purchase it. On-line Communities provide a prime opportunity for companies to get to know their customers more intimately and keep a finger on the pulse of their needs and behaviors. On-line communities offer a chance for companies to break down geographical barriers by connecting people globally in many different ways

**Figure 14 Product with devoted on-line fans: The Big Green Egg**

through on-line interaction. They allow for more detailed and sustained conversations and deepen customer relationships. They offer on-line interactive access for people, marketing collateral, information, and products.

One problem with on-line communities is that they are difficult to establish, and many are short-lived. Statistics describe the millions of members of Facebook, for example, without taking into account that hundreds of other sites have attempted to do the same thing and failed. Thriving on-line communities seem to have the following characteristics which enable them to endure:

◆ Don't cost the members any fees (i.e., are free) and don't have too much advertising.
◆ Are focused on hobbies and interests of people.
◆ Have long-term leaders who post frequently and keep everyone interested and civil.
◆ Focus on relationships, not information technology.
◆ Have enough of a base membership (at least 4,000) to maintain frequent postings of the 10 percent active readers and the 1 percent active posters.

Now that we have discussed the importance of e-strategy and noted the order in which businesses normally get involved in the Internet and the World Wide Web, let's move on to the applications that businesses utilize for websites, email, search engines, blogging and wikis.

## Websites

A website is a server application that runs on a physical server attached to the Internet. A list of web server software vendors and their market share as of April 2008 can be found in Table 8.[27] The web server waits for a request from a browser program such as Microsoft Internet Explorer, Mozilla Firefox, Open Source Opera, or Apple Safari. (Web browser market share can be found in Table 9.[28])

---

[27] Netcraft, an Internet research firm in Bath, England. http://survey.netcraft.com/Reports/200804/index.html posted in April, 2008, accessed in May of 2008.

[28] W3 Schools, a free on-line learning portal. http://www.w3schools.com/browsers/browsers_stats.asp from April 2008, accessed in May of 2008

**Table 8  Web server software & market share**

| Vendor | Product | Web Sites Hosted | Percent |
|--------|---------|------------------|---------|
| Open Source | Apache | 83,206,564 | 50.22% |
| Microsoft | IIS | 58,540,275 | 35.33% |
| Google | GWS | 10,075,991 | 6.08% |
| Oversee | Oversee | 1,926,812 | 1.16% |
| Others | - | 11,946,586 | 7.00% |

**Table 9 Web browsers (client software) and market share**

| Vendor | Product | Number of Users | Percent |
|--------|---------|-----------------|---------|
| Microsoft | Internet Explorer | 767,200,000 | 55% |
| Mozilla | Firefox | 561,400,000 | 40% |
| Apple | Safari | 30,800,000 | 2% |
| Open Source | Opera | 14,000,000 | 1% |

## How a Website Works

Here is how the world wide web works: The browser issues an HTTP command (hypertext transfer protocol) to request the display of a web page at a URL (universal resource locator). The webserver application responds by displaying the HTML (Hypertext markup language) stored in the file on the website at that URL.  Every click of the mouse on a hyperlink causes the same cycle to occur.

HTML is not really a full computer language because it does not have flow control command such as IF..NEXT or WHILE...DO.  The only thing HTML can do is place text and graphics and other objects (such as movies) on a web page to be rendered by a browser upon request.  You can see the HTML code by looking at any webpage in your browser and choosing to view the source code. Notice that HTML uses *tags,* identifiers surrounded with the less than (<) and greater than (>) symbols.  Tags normally have open tags and close tags, such as <head>  and </head> or <body> </body>.  To **boldface** a word, for example, it would have the opening bold tag and then a closing bold tag to turn off the bold, as in <bold> boldface </bold>.

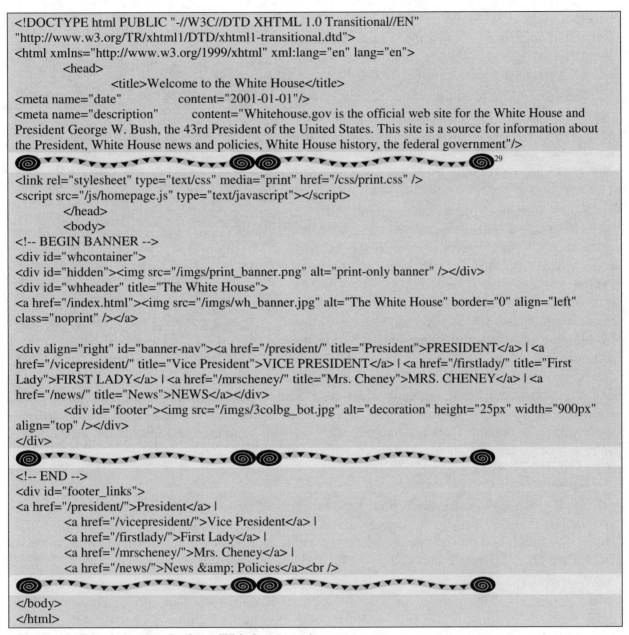

```
<!DOCTYPE html PUBLIC "-//W3C//DTD XHTML 1.0 Transitional//EN"
"http://www.w3.org/TR/xhtml1/DTD/xhtml1-transitional.dtd">
<html xmlns="http://www.w3.org/1999/xhtml" xml:lang="en" lang="en">
        <head>
                <title>Welcome to the White House</title>
<meta name="date"          content="2001-01-01"/>
<meta name="description"       content="Whitehouse.gov is the official web site for the White House and
President George W. Bush, the 43rd President of the United States. This site is a source for information about
the President, White House news and policies, White House history, the federal government"/>
```
29
```
<link rel="stylesheet" type="text/css" media="print" href="/css/print.css" />
<script src="/js/homepage.js" type="text/javascript"></script>
        </head>
        <body>
<!-- BEGIN BANNER -->
<div id="whcontainer">
<div id="hidden"><img src="/imgs/print_banner.png" alt="print-only banner" /></div>
<div id="whheader" title="The White House">
<a href="/index.html"><img src="/imgs/wh_banner.jpg" alt="The White House" border="0" align="left"
class="noprint" /></a>

<div align="right" id="banner-nav"><a href="/president/" title="President">PRESIDENT</a> | <a
href="/vicepresident/" title="Vice President">VICE PRESIDENT</a> | <a href="/firstlady/" title="First
Lady">FIRST LADY</a> | <a href="/mrscheney/" title="Mrs. Cheney">MRS. CHENEY</a> | <a
href="/news/" title="News">NEWS</a></div>
        <div id="footer"><img src="/imgs/3colbg_bot.jpg" alt="decoration" height="25px" width="900px"
align="top" /></div>
</div>
```
```
<!-- END -->
<div id="footer_links">
<a href="/president/">President</a> |
        <a href="/vicepresident/">Vice President</a> |
        <a href="/firstlady/">First Lady</a> |
        <a href="/mrscheney/">Mrs. Cheney</a> |
        <a href="/news/">News &amp; Policies</a><br />
```
```
</body>
</html>
```

**Figure 15  Sample html code (from Whitehouse.gov)**

One of the most common HTML commands is <a href ..../a>, which is the command to
display a hyperlink which jumps to another URL if someone clicks on it.  For example, <a
href="/firstlady/">First Lady</a> shows the word First Lady on the page, and if someone
clicks on it, that person will be taken to the URL http://www.whitehouse.gov/firstlady/.

---

[29] Curly line graphic denotes where text has been deleted so that you can see the beginning, middle, and end of the html
page.  Meta names are not displayed on the webpage, but are read by search engines.  The banner shows at the top of
the page and the footer shows at the bottom of the page.

(Normally the URL would have an actual file name, but in this case only the directory name, /firstlady/ is given. When that happens, the default web page is used, normally *index.html*.)

The other thing to notice about HTML is that it has no commands to interface with a database such as MySQL or Oracle. For that you need middleware such as PhP or Python or ASP (discussed in more detail in the Development Tools section of the Software chapter).

Many websites place the contents of the website inside a database, and then use middleware in order to dynamically write the HTML code when requested. Such sites are using a *content management system* (CMS). This makes it easier for the owners and authors of the website to make changes. CMSs also add the capability of allowing the reader to login so that access to

> **A single web page is thousands of packets**
> When you go on a web page and download a picture, for example, that picture is actually broken up into thousands of packets. Each individual packet might take a separate route to get back to your computer screen. Some might go through San Francisco while others travel through London and others travel through Tokyo. Some might only travel on local telephone links, while others might have gone through underwater cable links and still others travel via satellite. In the end, they all get to your PC and reassemble themselves into the proper order so that you can see the web page. The same thing happens with every single message and every single item that goes to or from every single webpage throughout the world every second of every minute of every day.

different parts of the site can be controlled. However, a CMS has two disadvantages; it slows down the website so that it takes longer for the browser to display the web page, and it means that the web page doesn't actually exist so a Search Engine like Google cannot find it. Nonetheless, CMSs makes the website much more manageable, and so they are becoming more and more popular. Choices include Microsoft Sharepoint, Oracle Portal, and dozens of open source systems including Mambo, Joomla, DotNetNuke, and WebGUI.

# Email

Email is unequivocally the "killer app" (a phrase that refers to the one most important application that "sells" a technology). Customers expect businesses to have email. With email, any individual person can send information to any other single person (as long as they know their email address). This is a powerful and essential business tool.

We rarely think about the actual process of getting an email message from our computers to the computer of the person for whom the email is intended. Don't think knowing how email works is important? I'm sure the business leaders at Anderson and Enron didn't think it was important either - until the email they thought they had deleted became the prime evidence against them (causing both organizations to go out of business and several leaders to go to jail). Knowing how email works is important for everyone.

## *How Email Works*

An email system needs a **sender** and a **receiver.** At each end, the sender needs to have an application that is capable of composing and addressing the message.

An email message has three components: the address, the @ sign, and the domain name. The address and the domains are separated by an @ symbol, as in "Mary@Tuffet.com". The user composes the message and addresses it using a program generically known as the *client email system*, which we will shorten to *email client*. The email client stores the message until it gets the instruction to send the message. When instructed, the email client connects with the *server email system* (or *email server)* and sends the message to it. The email server stores the message until it gets instructed to send it elsewhere. The email client of the user connects periodically with the email server, notices that a new message is stored in the mailbox of the user, and downloads the message so that the user can see that there is a new message. When the user sees the message, they can click on it to open it up and read it.

> **Story of the @ Symbol**
>
> Ray Tomlinson was one of the programmers working on figuring out how to transfer files over ARPANET (Advanced Research Projects Agency Network, the precursor of today's Internet) when it occurred to him that he could modify the SNDMSG (send message) command to attach files (i.e. an email). At the time, (in 1971) SNDMSG could only send a message from one user to another on the same machine. To attach files outside the system, he needed something to distinguish a local user mailbox from a mailbox on another computer. He noted that it seemed natural to use the @ sign, which was commonly used in commerce as in "6 baskets @ $2 each". In English, the sign was called "at", as in 6 baskets at 2 dollars each. Sending a message to "George" would send a local message, but sending a message to "George@Anothercomputer" would send it over ARPANET to another computer.

Underneath all Internet email systems is SMTP (*simple mail transfer protocol)* which contains the instructions for the email clients and email servers to deal with email messages. But on top of that you might have any one of thousands of configurations. Giving the names and publishers of email client software is difficult - it might be the same as the email server or it might be different. Some examples are:

- **Outlook Express** email client, **Qmail** email server.
- **Outlook** email client, **Exchange** email server.
- **Thunderbird** email client, **Netmail** email server.
- **Netscape** email client, **AOL** email server.
- **Eudora** email client, **Rockliffe** email server
- **Notes** email client, **Domino** email server

These examples list the software itself, not the publisher of the software or the provider of the email services. The email services might be provided by a company such as IBM or Walmart or BankAmerica. The email services might also be provided by a free website such as Google, or Yahoo, or MSN/Hotmail (Microsoft). It might also be provided by your Internet Service Provider (ISP) such as AOL, or Comcast, or Verizon. Or it might be provided by a company outsourcing it to a web hosting company or ISP. If the user uses a *web based email client*, then they can't really tell the difference between the email client and the email server because they both reside on the same computer and work together simultaneously - the email client might actually just be a form on a web page that provides a window into the messages stored on the web server.

## *Email Etiquette*

There is a large gap of knowledge between people who have been emailing for years and people who haven't been emailing for very long (or don't email often). It is difficult to know what the rules are because most of the rules for email etiquette are unwritten. Like an un-zipped fly or bad breath, few email recipients will say anything if we break the unwritten rules, (though they may laugh at us behind our backs).

In some cases, the problem stems from not realizing that rules for business-oriented emails are different from rules for informal social emails. If you are emailing a friend, there's no problem with shortcuts, text codes, poor grammar or spelling. As long as your friend understands the message, you can pretty much write whatever you want.

However, when we use social email rules for business communication, it's like showing up at a business mixer in jeans and a T-shirt where everyone else is wearing a suit. No one will complain, but neither will they take us very seriously. Here are some of the unwritten rules for professional email. See how many of them you already know.

- ♦ Use a meaningful topic in the subject line.
- ♦ Begin with a greeting.
- ♦ End with a signature.
- ♦ Use good grammar.
- ♦ Use the spell checker.
- ♦ Don't use ALL CAPS.
- ♦ Use a professional email address.
- ♦ Properly configure your email program with your real name.
- ♦ Share your email address; put it on your business card.
- ♦ Deal with spam professionally.
- ♦ Avoid emotionless email escalation.
- ♦ Use CC or BC judiciously to copy others.
- ♦ Only turn on request receipts if you can restrict them to internal email.
- ♦ Only configure out of office messages if you can restrict them to internal email.
- ♦ Don't use an email distribution list as a discussion board.
- ♦ Don't send jokes, virus warnings, or other extraneous information.
- ♦ Don't write anything in an email you wouldn't want to see written on the first page of The New York Times.

An email message is just like a business letter; impressions count. When you don't use a meaningful subject line, or you skip the greeting and signature, you are conveying the underlying message that the recipient of your email is not very important to you. If you use poor spelling or grammar, you are further portraying yourself as uneducated or unintelligent. Additionally, using all capital letters conveys the impression THAT YOU ARE YELLING AT THE TOP OF YOUR LUNGS AT THE PERSON TO WHOM YOU ARE WRITING, which does not convey the calm thoughtful person you would probably prefer to convey.

While it may be fun to use ChickInHeat@Hotmail.com or PhillyFan@aol.com, your business communication will not be seen as professional. Also, if you don't fill in the "Name" field of your email program, you make a bad impression. Take the extra step and set up your real name. (Send yourself an email to see how it looks to others when you send them an email, and if your real name appears in the From line.)

One of the downsides of email is spam (unwanted bulk email). Even worse, emails can be [gasp!] fraudulent and filled with lies. Phishing is the name given to an email that tries to elicit private information from you for nefarious purposes such as stealing your money or identity. Experienced emailers quickly learn to ignore anything that sounds too good to be true. (No, you did not really win the Irish Lottery, and you haven't really been offered a percentage of the $30 million that some expelled Nigerian king would like to transfer to your U.S. bank account.)

But spam and phishing can be dealt with professionally. First, don't be a whiner. Don't complain about spam. Spam is not going to go away. Railing against it is like railing against the humidity. Just like junk mail, accept that every day you will have to quickly look through all your messages and delete most of them because they are unwanted bulk messages not addressed to you. Learn to use your spam filter and don't respond to spam or phishing.

Why is spam filtering so hard? Like junk mail, spam is in the eye of the beholder. The most common definition for spam is "unsolicited email," but that definition doesn't work. If I send a "how are you doing" message to my sister in California, it was unsolicited, but no one would call it spam. "Unsolicited bulk email" doesn't work either. If I send the same message to all my friends and family with email addresses, the number is well over 200 (I have a very big family). But again—no one would call it spam (though many anti-spam programs would refuse it because it is addressed to more than 50 names at one time).

In business, if you send a newsletter to 300 people that you know and have met personally even if they didn't ask for it, that is not spam. If you send the same newsletter to 30,000 people, most of whom you've never met, that is spam. If you send a "how are you doing" message to 300,000 people, it would definitely be spam no matter what the content. But if the IRS sends out 2 million emails to people to let them know some information they need to get their refunds, that would not be spam no matter how many people receive it.

Unwanted bulk email is, by definition, based on a human judgment (unwanted). While a human being can look at any message and pretty much figure out immediately if it is unwanted, a computer cannot. As a result, your email messages to others may get caught in the spam filter. When sending an important email, always follow up with a phone call so that the recipient can get the message out of the spam bucket if it landed there. Never assume that someone has read your email. And most important, don't send spam.

Also remember that email has the tendency to come across very harsh and aggressive. Normally, over 90 percent of a message's intent comes from facial expression and tone of voice, which doesn't exist in email. When receiving a negative-sounding email, reply by phone or a personal visit, not a reply email. If it is from someone you do not know, ignore it.

Be judicious in copying others on your email communications, and circumspect in the topics you choose to email. Filling in the CC: (carbon copy—and yes it is an anachronism) seems like a quick and efficient way to copy third parties on an email message. But copying can be a problem. You don't know how the recipient will react to your copying someone else on the message.

Blind copy (BC:) can also get you in trouble. Blind copy hides the email addresses of the people receiving the email. One legitimate reason to use blind copy is to avoid annoying the reader with a long list of email addresses (through which they must scroll) before they get to the message. Another legitimate reason to use blind copy is when you are sending to a confidential list of people. The Society for Information Management sends out a monthly email to all their members, for example, but they don't want any of the vendor members to use the list for promotional offers, so they properly send it out as a blind copy.

The problem occurs when you use blind copy to hide the fact that someone was copied on the message. That's risky by itself, but it is even riskier if you don't communicate with the person who was copied. They may very well forward (or reply all) to the message—letting the original target person know that you've been duplicitous. It's better not to use blind copy to hide the fact that the message has been copied, but if you do, ensure that the recipient knows why you sent it as a blind copy. Alternatively, if you receive a message without your email address in the To: or CC: fields, treat the message as confidential, and do not forward or reply.

Only turn on request receipts if you can restrict them to internal email. A receipt request is a request that goes out to the recipient of an email that requests a return message to let the sender know that the recipient received or read the message. The problem is that receipt request does not work well if the recipient is on a different network, a different email system, or if the sender sends the message to the recipient's internet email account. Instead of being convenient and under the covers, the recipients would get a second email that asks for a reply whether or not they've read the original message—redundant and annoying for the receiver of such a request. Being able to tell if someone has gotten your email sounds like a good idea, but since it can't be implemented without annoying the recipient of the email, it's better just to leave the feature turned off.

Only configure out of office messages if you can restrict them to internal email. An out of office message is a response to every email you receive that says something like "I'll be out of office message from July 3 to July 16 and will respond to your email when I've returned." I've heard the arguments for using out of office messages: " I want people to know that I'm on vacation, that I'm not ignoring their emails." Unfortunately, the distribution nature of email means that you often get emails that are directed at a group, not just you. An email distribution list is a single email address to which an email can be sent once, but is received by dozens or hundreds or thousands of people. Out of office messages are even more annoying when the email list is configured to reply back to all members of the list. If you've ever been a member of an on-line community email list, you probably have seen messages from other members who keep turning on their out of office message. Every time they go on vacation, all the people on the list who don't know them (and even more importantly, don't care about them) find out they are going on vacation. Furthermore, when your system replies to a message that's been sent by a spammer, they get confirmation that there's a real live person on the other end of that email address, and the value of your email address among spammers just quadrupled—as will the amount of spam that you get.

The fact is, email (alone) is not appropriate for information of a time-sensitive nature. Since there is no guarantee that people will see your email in time (or even at all) it makes more sense to use the phone for time-sensitive issues, and expect others to do the same. Therefore, in most industries the appropriate place for information about when you are on vacation is voice mail. The news only goes to the people who are actively trying to reach you, and doesn't go out to the hundreds of people who might not care.

Also remember that email distribution lists are meant to foster communication among various people who need to communicate some important information. A problem occurs when people don't realize that they receive a message from a distribution list and they treat it as if it were a personal email. Invariably, someone who is unfamiliar with email distribution lists will hit the reply button and say something like "I missed you at the meeting last night. Give me a call and we can get together and talk about George."

Not quite as bad image-wise, but sometimes even more annoying, is the tendency for people to send out their opinion to the whole distribution list (as if everyone else wants to know what they think). Of course, if the purpose of the email distribution list is to be used as a discussion board, then this behavior is not only okay, it is encouraged. But if the email distribution list is meant for important announcements, then for various people to use it as a sounding board will lower its value as an attention-getting device.

A sure sign that someone is inexperienced in email is the sending of jokes, virus warnings, or other items that they have been urged to send to everyone they know. The reason this behavior shows their inexperience is because anyone who's been using email professionally for more than a few years has already seen all of the jokes, virus warnings, and feel-good emails.

Finally, be careful what you write in email. Some people have the idea that email should be private. Perhaps this mistaken notion stems from the federal laws against tampering with U.S. postal mail. (In 1792 Congress imposed the death penalty for that crime!) But in this way email is very different from postal mail. Email can be read in plain text by anyone with a particular network device as it travels over the public Internet. Furthermore, email is possessed by the owners of several servers through which it passes on its journey from writer to recipient. Those servers may be backed up several times throughout the day, resulting in several permanent copies of any email message. Instead of thinking of email as a sealed letter, think of it like a postcard. There is literally no way to keep an email private. By the way—the same is true for IMing (instant messaging or chatting). So think before you text and send.

### *Proliferation of Email Addresses*

It is common for a single individual to have dozens of different email addresses (even if they don't use them all.) Let's take an example; Joe Schmoe.

Joe Schmoe graduated from Central High School. Because he is an active Alumni, the school assigned him an email address, JoeSchmoe@CentralHS.edu. Joe also got his bachelor's degree from Big State University, so he is also SchmJ2134@BSU.edu. When he started his Master's degree, he got JSCHM112@HigherLearning.edu.

His local ISP is Comcast, so he also has Schmoe.Joe@comcast.net, and his work email is JosephSchmoe@GIManufacturing.com. When he was looking for a job he used Big-

Man@MSN.net, and when he joined a group about weight lifting (one of his hobbies), he got BigLifter@Yahoo.com. One of his suppliers put him on a workteam that is using joint documents on Google, so he also has Engineer@Gmail.com. He is also very active in his church, who assigned him the email LeadUsher@SaintJohn.org. When he became the Treasurer of his hunting lodge, he also became Treasurer@HuntersRus.org.

Joe can handle this proliferation in a number of ways: manually checking each one, forwarding each one, or automatically checking each one.

Joe can check the messages at each one of the ten different addresses. At work, the IT people set up Outlook for him, so he goes into that to check his GIManufacturing messages. At home he uses Outlook Express to check his Comcast email. The people at his church gave him the instructions for using Thunderbird to check his SaintJohn messages, so that's the program he uses to check that email. Each of the others has set up a web client, so he goes to the web page of each of the other six addresses to check his messages.

The problem with this method is that checking so many different email servers is a lot of work. Joe usually doesn't keep up, and weeks can go by before he gets a message at one of the more remote email servers. Eventually he will probably stop checking them altogether. He may end up asking everyone to send him messages at BigMan@MSN.net because that one he checks every day or so. But even that is a problem. The other email servers are holding onto his email messages, but since he never goes in and checks them, the mailbox fills up until it consumes all of the space he is allowed (his quota) and then starts *bouncing* (which means that anyone who sends a message gets a return message saying that the message couldn't be delivered because the mailbox was full - which leaves a very bad impression and conveys laziness.)

Alternatively, Joe can *forward* (which means to issue the instruction to each of the email servers to send any messages they receive to another email address) to his "main" email address. Let's say, in this case, most people know his address as BigMan@MSN.net, so he sets all the other addresses to forward to that one. This method is better than the first, although doesn't always work. AOL email, for example, does not have a forwarding feature. Furthermore, people send to one email address, but get a reply from a different email address, which is confusing for them.

## *Setting up an Email Client for Multiple Email Addresses*

Joe could handle the problem in a different way. Instead of going to each of the ten different email servers using the email client the technical people described, Joe could also decide which email client he wants to use and set it up to go to all the different email servers and pick up his mail. To do this he would use an email client such as Outlook that has this capability (not all email clients do). In the Tools menu he would set up a different account for each of his ten email addresses. He enters in the setup screen for each email account the name of the email server, his email name, and whatever password he uses to access that email. Then, when he clicks on "Send/Receive", Outlook goes out to each of the email servers and downloads the messages. To set up all his email accounts, he would need to understand the four different ways that email clients can connect to email servers.

- **Direct connection** -for example, Exchange and Domino are both email servers that can connect directly with clients that were designed specifically for the purpose.

- **HTTP** - (Hypertext Transfer Protocol) connection through a web server onto a web page. Email messages stay on the web page and is viewed as if going to the website.

- **IMAP** - (Internet Message Access Protocol) connection through an Internet site into your email client. Email messages *synchronize* but do not *download*. They remain on the server until you delete them there.

- **POP3** - (Post Office Protocol) normal connection between an email server and an email client. Email is downloaded, and only stays on the server if you have configured the settings to leave the messages there after downloading.

Often, the IT people who set up the email servers provide choices for the people who are connecting their email clients. (If they haven't, you must choose the one recommended by the IT people who set up the email server.) POP3 provides the most flexibility in terms of storing and retrieving messages from a single personal computer. The messages get downloaded and you can put them into folders, read them even when you are not connected, easily move them to another location, and make sure they are backed up.

On the other hand, if you travel a lot or prefer to be able to see all your messages from any machine at any location, IMAP or HTTP are better choices because the messages stay on the server. The disadvantage is that you can't read the messages if you are not connected to the Internet. Also - you are relying upon the provider to backup the messages, and it is very difficult to move them to another service provider because they are physically stored on a server you don't own or have administrative access to.

Additionally, reading email with a web email client is not as flexible as reading email with a PC-based email client. For example, if you have 90,000 messages over the past year and want to find one that was sent to you from BigGirl@yahoo.com on January 20th, you can easily set up those search parameters in Outlook for the messages that are stored on your hard drive. You can't search that specifically on a web client. You can also more easily set up folders and rules on messages stored on your PC.

Regardless of how many email addresses you have, it makes sense for any business person to learn how to effectively manage their email[30]. Now that we've covered the basics of websites and email, let's discuss a few other important applications and websites on the World Wide Web.

## Search Engines

A search engine is a site where people go to find other sites (a more generic form of an aggregating site). The most popular search engine site today is Google.com (unless you are Chinese, in which case Baidu.com is the most popular), but in past years Ask.com, Yahoo.com, MSN.com and AltaVista.com have all made a run for top status, although none have attained the popularity of Google.

---

[30] You can take an on-line course in effective email management at http://eganemailsolutions.com/

How do search engines list their sites? Well, the answer is constantly changing. The work involved in getting a high profile on the search engine listings led to a whole new industry—search engine optimization (SEO). Anyone considering putting a new Web site up may get inundated with sales pitches from SEO consultants. SEOs keep up with the latest changes in how search engines work.

For example, in the past, the more keyword meta tags embedded in a site, the higher the chance that the site would appear in the search list. At time went by, however, search engines took notice of people focusing only on keywords. They changed the rules so that sites that had *too many* keywords on each page became disqualified.

At the present time, the following items influence the placement on Google:[31]

- ♦ Search term use in title tag, headings, and body text.
- ♦ Relationship of body text content to search terms (topic analysis).
- ♦ Global link popularity of site (how many other sites link to yours).
- ♦ Age of site and document (the older the better).
- ♦ Amount of indexable text content (more text, less graphics).
- ♦ Frequency of updates to page (the more frequent the better).
- ♦ Documents not too deep (less than four folders in the path).
- ♦ Accuracy of spelling and grammar (no misspellings or errors).
- ♦ Well-designed code (no coding errors).

## Blogging & Wikis

As discussed in the section on collaboration in the software chapter, a weblog (often shortened to simply blog) is a web page where a person can post their opinion. Unlike on-line discussion boards where many people both post and read what is posted, a blog is a web page where one primary person posts (though complicated by the fact that most blogging software includes a reply capabilities so that readers can read and comment on the blog). A discussion board is where everyone chimes in, whereas a blog is more like one person "holding court" and responding to each comment.

When blogs first became popular, there were only a few thousand and the freedom of being able to post in a world-wide venue whatever you wanted without worrying about censorship or editing was a bit of an innovation. People didn't have to host their own web site to be able to post their ideas. Then traditional media such as newspapers, radio, and television started to take advantage of blogs to extend their own reach. As more and more people began to create blogs, the amount of poorly-written uninteresting material began to drown out the insightful blogs. At this point there are hundreds of thousands of blogs, and the novelty has worn thin. Successful busy people rarely have the time necessary to post frequently. Furthermore, for anyone who reads many blogs, it becomes quickly apparent that there is a role for editing even in cyberspace. Although blogs are still relatively popular

---

[31] Fishkin , R., and J. Pollard. 2007. *Search engine ranking factors*. http://www.seomoz.org/article/search-ranking-factors#f3 (accessed June 8, 2007).

(especially when the blog application is combined with an on-line community), as a separate entity blogs are likely to fade out in the next few years.

Wikis, on the other hand, are proving to be much more popular and robust as they serve a larger need than providing a place for people to state their own opinions. Similar to blogging, a wiki is a web application that enables people to post information without *direct* editorial oversight. I say *direct* because anyone on a wiki can post anything as well as *edit* anything already posted. Wikipedia has proven a success because of an almost-militant dedication to ensuring that the information posted is free from bias. If someone posts something that is obviously biased, someone else will come along and change the post. Every post, and every change to every post, is logged so that people can see what is going on. The type of web application software used by Wikipedia is available on many other sites (or available for download on your own website). Wikimatrix.org is a website that compares over a hundred different wikis available. The most popular wikis are Wikispaces, MediaWiki, DoKuWiki, PmWiki, WikkiTikkiTavi, PhpWiki, and TWiki.

Now that we've discussed many different applications that run on the Internet, let's discuss the details of what, exactly, is meant by the Internet.

# Chapter 6: Internetworking

As noted earlier, the Internet is a world-wide network of connected computers. What makes the Internet the Internet is that every one of those computers is using the same Transmission Control Protocol on top of the same Internet Protocol (TCP/IP).

## Internet Protocol

At one time there were many networking protocols. Microsoft used NetBEUI (NetBIOS Extended User Interface). Novell Netware used IPX/SPX. But TCP/IP has become so ubiquitous at the internetworking level that all the other protocols have taken a back seat or have been discontinued.

There are several characteristics of Internet technologies that combine to form what we know of as the Internet. They are: mesh topology, ip addressing, routing, subnetting, Domain Name Servers (DNS), and Dynamic Host Configuration Protocol (DHCP).

### Mesh Topology

The Internet is based upon a mesh topology. The mesh topology utilizes many-to-many links (with each "node" connected to all or some other nodes, as illustrated in Figure 16). This topology was developed so that even if a whole section of the internetwork were damaged, the internetwork as a whole would still be connected.

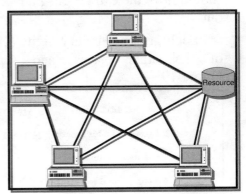

**Figure 16 Simple mesh toplogy**

### IP Address

In an internet, each computer or device is connected to each other computer or device, as can be seen in the illustration of the Internet mesh in Figure 17. Each device is identified through a unique number called an IP address (Internet Protocol address). In the Internet, all of the numbers are centrally controlled and managed.

An IP address is comprised of a 32-bit number (32 digits in binary notation), although normally it is represented in a special format known as dotted decimal notation. Dotted decimal notation breaks the 32 digits into 4 groups of 8. This conveniently allows one byte (normally 8 digits in binary

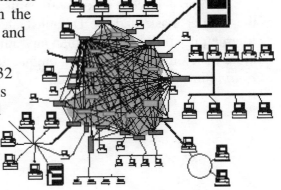

**Figure 17  The Internet mesh**

notation, which is also referred to as an octet) to represent each group.

To translate from each group of 8-bit binary digits to the decimal number, each bit is given a value that corresponds to its location in the string. For example if the binary code was 11111111, then the first value would be 128, the second value would be 64, etc. You can see 2 binary numbers translated in Figure 18.

| 1 | 1 | 1 | 1 | 1 | 1 | 1 | 1 | |
|---|---|---|---|---|---|---|---|---|
| 128 | 64 | 32 | 16 | 8 | 4 | 2 | 1 = 255 | |

| 0 | 1 | 0 | 1 | 0 | 1 | 0 | 1 | |
|---|---|---|---|---|---|---|---|---|
| 0 | 64 | 0 | 16 | 0 | 4 | 0 | 1 = 85 | |

**Figure 18 Translating from binary to decimal**

You add the values together (128+64+32+16+8+4+2+1) and you get 255, the largest possible value for an IP address. In Figure 19, the binary number 10000111 translates to 135, the number 00001111 translates to 15, the number 00000010 translates to 2, and 00011110 translates to 30. Note that it is not entirely standardized whether the dotted decimal notation should have the extra digits padded, as shown above, and many people just leave the padding out.

Each group of binary digits (bits) is then converted into decimal notation independently of the other places, and separated with dots (decimal points), as shown in Figure 19.

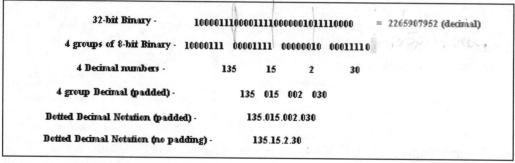

**Figure 19 Dotted Decimal Notation**

A computer needs to know three items in order to connect to the Internet; the IP address, the Subnet mask, and the Default Gateway. The IP Address is unique - if you are on the Internet, it will be different than any other computer in the world. The IP address does much more than simply identifying a unique device, however. The IP address actually provides the *routing* information for a packet.

*ipconfig. | Local Area Connection Status*

## Routing

The Default Gateway is another name for the *router*. The default gateway that is listed when you issue the IPCONFIG command is the nearest router to your computer. A router is the device that connects you to the Internet; think of it like a door to the Internet. Every computer must have a router to connect, (although many people on the same network will undoubtedly have the same router).

A router has a specific task; when a router receives a packet, it reads the destination IP address and send the packet in the direction of the destination (i.e. routes the packet). A router does not necessarily send them on the best or quickest

> **Looking at your IP address**
>
> If you get into the command line on your computer (on a Windows machine you can choose the DOS Prompt from the Accessory menu, or type CMD after choosing the Run command on the main menu), you can type in IPCONFIG. The system will display three items: the IP address, the Subnet mask, and the Default Gateway.
>
> Keep in mind that your IP address may change each time that you reboot your computer. Your system may be set up to be assigned an IP address as soon as it attempts to connect to the Internet.

path, it will just pick a path from among the list of other routers that will get the packet closer. Each time a packet gets read by a router on the Internet, it *hops* to the next router until it finally reaches a router that is actually directly attached to the computer with the destination IP address. You can see the trace route to ebay.com from a computer in Ashburn, Virginia in Figure 20 showing the hops. Notice that the packet travelled from VA to DC to AZ back to DC and then to Denver, Colorado (where eBay's servers must be connected to the Internet). Notice also that the packet went across five different networks on its way. Ten hops is pretty good; more than 30 would have been pretty bad. Also notice that the packet got "hung up" at the 6th and 9th hop; either the routers were too busy to deal with the packet right away, or they were not working properly. Nonetheless, the delay was still so fast (53 milliseconds is 53/1000 of a second) that we would barely notice it..[32]

---

[32] The utility that will provide the tracert can be downloaded from http://visualroute.visualware.com/, although you can also type in *tracert ebay.com* from any command line or DOS prompt.

| | | Connection test for ebay.com completed | | | | | |
|---|---|---|---|---|---|---|---|

View: **Summary** | **Table** | **Performance Graph** | **Analysis** | **Map**

| Hop | %loss | IP Address | Node Name | Location | ms | Graph | Network |
|---|---|---|---|---|---|---|---|
| 0 | 0 | 205.234.111.204 | DTG311.visualwa | *Ashburn, VA, US/* | - | | Defender Technol |
| 1 | 0 | 205.234.111.129 | r03-8.iad.defende | Washington, DC, | 0 | | Defender Technol |
| 2 | 0 | 69.65.112.25 | r01.iad.defenderh | Washington, DC, | 9 | | Defender Technol |
| 3 | 0 | 69.28.158.173 | ve103.fr4.iad.llnw | Washington, DC, | 0 | | Limelight Network |
| 4 | 0 | 69.28.171.213 | ve5.fr3.iad.llnw.ne | Washington, DC, | 1 | | Limelight Network |
| 5 | 0 | 64.215.26.125 | TenGigabitEthern | *Phoenix, AZ, USA* | 0 | | Global Crossing ( |
| 6 | 0 | 64.208.110.30 | qwest-1.ar2.DCA: | Washington, DC, | 41 | | Global Crossing ( |
| 7 | 0 | 205.171.251.61 | dcx-core-02.inet.q | Washington, DC, | 1 | | Qwest Communic |
| 9 | 0 | 205.171.10.78 | dvr-edge-03.inet.c | Denver, CO, USA | 53 | | Qwest Communic |
| 10 | - | 66.135.221.11 | pages.ebay.com | - | - | | eBay Inc EBAY-1 |

**Figure 20 Trace route showing hops to Ebay.com**

Sometimes the packet doesn't get where it is going. Each packet on the Internet has a TTL (Time To Live) counter. When the TTL counter runs out, the packet stops looking for its destination (i.e. the routers stop forwarding the packet). The sending application never receives the expected acknowledgement packet, so it simply sends the data out again.

The key to routing is the IP address itself. Notice in Figure 20 that when the packet went from Phoenix to Washington DC, it was still n the same network (which you can tell from the network number 64 that starts the IP address). Notice in Figure 21 that the IP addresses of the routers (the small gray boxes) begin the same as all the devices connected to the router. In order for the router to figure out exactly which numbers will be the same and which ones will differ, the router needs to know the *subnet mask*. The subnet mask was the middle number in the IPCONFIG information, and needs to be explained.

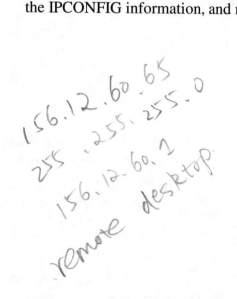

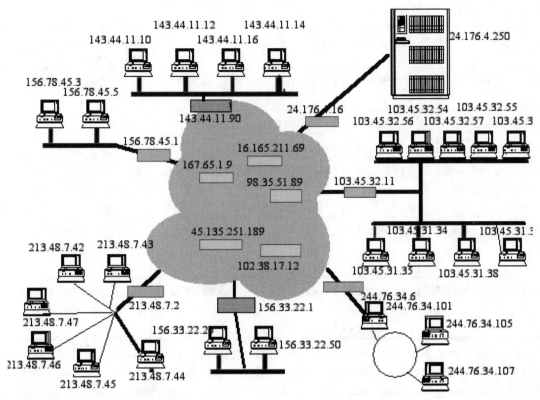

**Figure 21 IP Addresses on Internet**

## *Sub-netting*

The 32-bit IP address identifies a specific device on a specific network. Since the intent is to route the message to the correct network for delivery to the destination device (also called a host or node), it is helpful to clearly demarcate which part of the address indicates the network, and which part identifies the node on the network. The "assigned IP address" is assigned by the Internet Service Provider (ISP) (who in turn had received their assigned IP addresses from the Network Information Center). But the IP address assigned only indicates the network portion of an IP address. It is up to local administration of the ISP to assign specific addresses within the contiguous group to individual nodes.

To identify how many digits refer to the network and how many can be assigned to individual nodes, sub-networks are set up within the address area. Essentially, additional bits of the address (normally used for host identification) are dedicated to network identification. Only systems within the address area are "aware", however, that the assigned address indicates multiple networks. The routers within the network, for example, must be aware of the proper subnetwork to route a packet to, so they must be configured with a network (or subnetwork) mask. The mask indicates which digits are used for network and subnetwork identification, and which are used for host identification. The way that the subnet addresses are assigned can be seen in Table 10.

**Table 10  Assigning Subnet Masks**

| Type | Dotted binary notation | Dotted Decimal Notation |
| --- | --- | --- |
| Original address assigned | 10000000.11111001.00000000.00000000 | 128.249.000.000 |
| Network mask | 11111111.11111111.00000000.00000000 | 255.255.0.0 |
| Subnet mask | 11111111.11111111.11100000.00000000 | 255.255.224.0 |
| Subnet 1 addresses | 11111111.11111001.00100000.00000000 to 11111111.11111001.00111111.11111111 | 128.249.000.001 to 128.249.063.255 |
| Subnet 2 addresses | 11111111.11111001.01000000.00000000 to 11111111.11111001.01011111.11111111 | 128.249.064.000 to 128.249.95.255 |
| Subnet 3 addresses | 11111111.11111001.10000000.00000000 to 11111111.11111001.10011111.11111111 | 128.249.128.000 to 128.249.159.255 |

Basically, network administrators can set up the number of networks and the number of devices any way they want. A subnet mask of 255.0.0.0 will give you 125 networks and 16,777,214 devices. A subnet mask of 255.255.0.0 will give you 16,382 networks and 65,534 devices. A subnet mask of 255.255.255.0 (the most common in corporations) will give you 2,097,152 networks and 254 devices. From the perspective of the user, it does not matter which subnet mask the network administrator has set up as long as all the machines on the same subnet are using the same subnet mask. If you change any of the numbers shown in the IPConfig, you will no longer be able to connect to the Internet (or to any other computer on the subnet).

To recap: every computer on the Internet has a unique number, and the subnet mask tells each computer and each router where it exists in the hierarchy of networks and devices. When a computer wishes to send information to another computer, it breaks up the information into smaller pieces and encapsulates them into a packet. It includes within the packet both the source IP address and the destination IP address. Then it sends the packet to the default gateway (i.e. the nearest router). The router reads the destination IP address and sends the packet towards the network that contains that IP address.

But wait a minute. How does the computer know what IP address to put into the packet in the first place? We, as human beings, don't go around memorizing the IP addresses of every web sit we wish to visit. Nor do we have at the tip of our tongues the IP addresses of the people to whom we wish to send emails. Somehow the computer must have a way of figuring out how to translate JoeSchmoe@kutztown.edu into 156.12.1.115 and http://yahoo.com into 206.190.60.37.

## Domain Name Servers (DNS)

A computer can look up the IP address of any domain name by sending a message to the nearest Domain Name Server (DNS) and asking where it can find the domain. The Domain Name Server responds with the IP address. Any web address you type into the browser, any hyperlink you click on, any email message you try to send; they all require that the words be translated into IP addresses.

> **Finding out your DNS**
>
> If you go back to the command prompt on your computer and type in IPCONFIG /ALL (the same command as before but this time asking for all of the information instead of just some of the information), you will be able to see your DNS, since it will be listed. Like your IP address, your DNS may change depending upon your ISP.

There are thousands of DNSs on the Internet. The DNSs each have a list of every IP address and its corresponding domain name. Each DNS also gets updated from the other DNSs frequently - every few minutes or so. That way, even as domains are being registered or expired or changed by their hosting companies, all the DNSs in the world will know about the change within a few hours.

Most of the time your computer will list two or three different DNSs in case the first one is busy or out of commission. If your DNS address is not configured correctly, then you will be able to connect to the Internet, but you won't be able to find any web pages or click on any hyperlinks.

You may be wondering how your computer gets the IP address and the DNS address. Sometimes you may be directed by your ISP or corporation to type them into the TCP/IP options. But most of the time, we get the IP address, the subnet mask, and the DNS from our ISP through a process called DHCP (Dynamic Host Configuration Protocol).

## Dynamic Host Configuration Protocol (DHCP)

DHCP is the process that provides your computer with needed information to connect to the Internet. When your computer is turned on, it usually doesn't have an IP address. (If it did, that would be known as a *static* IP address. Your ISP would have directed you to type in the IP address, the subnet mask, and the DNS address.) Most computers are assigned this information when they initially try to connect to the Internet.

This is how DHCP works. The OS sends out a message (to any other device that is listening since at this point the computer doesn't know where the router is) that is the electronic equivalent of "I am here". Somewhere on the network (usually the router, but not always) there will be a DHCP program listening for that message. When it hears it, DHCP responds "Hi, how ya doin', Here's your IP address, your subnet mask, your default gateway, and your DNS." The OS stores the information and uses it the next time it wants to communicate with any other computer on the Internet. Once assigned, this information stays the same until the computer is turned off. You can see what the settings look like if your computer is using DHCP by looking in Figure 22. If your computer has a static IP address, then the options would be filled in rather than being set to **Obtain IP address automatically** and **Obtain DNS server address automatically.**

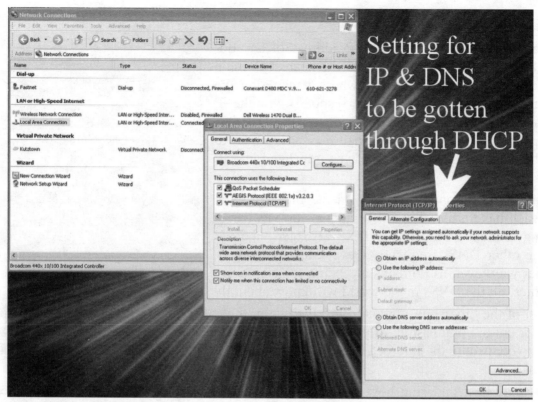

**Figure 22 DHCP configuration**

Now that we have fully covered the Internetworking concepts, let's move down one more layer; to the physical networking layer.

# Chapter 7: Networking

Many business people (from novice students to hapless CEOs) have a general understanding about personal computers because they've begun to use them regularly. Terms like mouse and menu and icon are easily understood by almost everyone these days.

The same cannot be said for networking. For most people, how information gets from the personal computers in our homes and businesses to other people's homes and businesses is a complete mystery - a black box. It seems to work like magic - until it breaks. Then suddenly we are left without the basic information we need to figure out if we should call the phone company, the device manufacturer, or the PC help desk.

More importantly, if we don't know the difference between a local area network (LAN) and a wide area network (WAN) when we are making information technology decisions, we could waste millions of dollars. (See the inset story on The Saga of the Publishing On Demand Application over a LAN and a WAN.)

---

### The Saga of the Publishing On Demand Application over a LAN and a WAN

Once upon a time there was a publishing company who needed help with a publish-on-demand project. The vendor of the software promised them that they could send large files (more than 20 megabytes) from one part of the company to another part of the company a few blocks away instantaneously. The publishing company paid millions of dollars for this system to be developed, and the project manager (PM) was coming in on the back end to ensure that the pilot system could be tested before the full implementation.

Well, after troubleshooting and fixing many problems (including the wrong bios installed on the computers in the lab and the wrong cables used to connect), the PM finally came up against a problem the PM couldn't fix. The developers of the software (who were programmers, not networking experts) did not understand the difference between a LAN and a WAN. They had thought that a 20 megabyte file being sent across a wide area network would not take any longer than a 20 megabyte file being sent across a local area network. The vendor had two different buildings, several blocks apart with a local area connection between those two buildings (possible because the vendor owned all the land between the two buildings and were able to lay a trunk cable to extend their network). The developers working for the vendor used the LAN as they did their programming.

The publishing company customer also had two different buildings several blocks apart - but the customer was missing that ever-important underground trunk cable. So, instead of a local area network transmitting at 10 or 100 megabits per second, the publishing company was planning on using this application over a wide area network transmitting at 1.5 megabits per second (the speed of the T-1 line they leased from the phone company).

Well, the PM figured out pretty early on that the application simply wouldn't work across a wide area connection. A twenty megabyte file can transmit across a local area network in a few seconds. That 20 megabyte file traveling on a 1.5 megabits per second line would take almost an hour to transmit. The software would stop waiting for the file and disconnect long before it was fully transmitted, so the pilot test failed.

# Local Area Network (LAN)

A local area network (LAN) is a network within a limited geographic area; most usually within a single building, but could also be within a campus or a number of connected homes. LANs are very fast, ranging from 2 megabits per second to 100 megabits per second.

While the top speeds of WANs are approaching the speeds of the slowest local area networks, there is still a big gap between the different types of networks. College campuses and businesses who own the ground between their buildings (and therefore can lay their own cables) can set up huge local area networks. Cable companies can also set up local area networks within a single neighborhood, as they do when they sell broadband cable data service.

You can see an illustration of a local area network spanning two buildings in Figure 23.

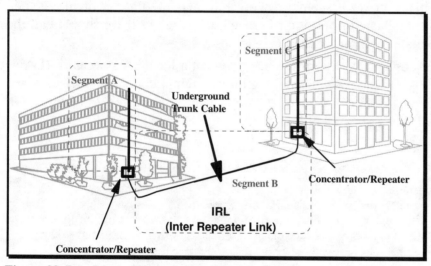

**Figure 23  Local Area Network that Spans Buildings**

Confusion between LANs and WANs may one day disappear;  WAN links will eventually get as large and as fast as local area network links, but in general WANs are still significantly slower than LANs.  A software program written for a LAN cannot be run over a WAN (although any program written for a WAN can be used on a LAN).

The difference between a LAN and a WAN is established by whether the transmission is *broadband* or *baseband*, which type of devices (*switches* or *routers*) are used to do the connection, and which *protocol* is in use on the network.

## *Broadband and Baseband*

When sending a signal across a wire, two schemes can be used; *broadband* or *baseband*. The majority of local area networks use baseband signaling, although some systems do use broadband, particularly for long range communication, or those which may suffer from higher than normal interference (such as in an industrial environment).

Broadband indicates that the information is used to *modulate* (varying the frequency or amplitude) of a *carrier* signal or frequency. In broadband signaling, it is the differences in the basic (carrier) signal which carries the information.

Baseband signaling does not use a separate carrier signal. The data itself is the only signal transmitted on the wire, and therefore is the carrier. Figure 24 illustrates the difference between broadband and baseband signaling. It should be apparent that a cable for a broadband signal must have a much higher bandwidth, since it must carry both the low frequency data modulation and the high frequency carrier. A baseband transmission cable needs to handle only the frequencies of the data encoding signal.

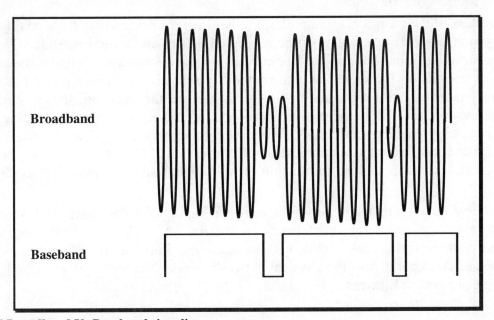

**Figure 24 Broadband Vs Baseband signaling**

However, the use of modulation in broadband transmissions allows the signal to travel much longer distances, since the power of an electrical signal is linked to the frequency. The higher the frequency of the highest signal (the carrier), the more power the signal will have.

Consider the reverse concept: lower frequency signals require less power. Since, as noted earlier, the thicker a conductor is, the higher the frequency it can carry, therefore, if you want to transmit a high frequency signal which does not require a great amount of power to generate, then you simply have to use thicker conductors. (Power versus thickness will become clearer when we explain cabling later in this chapter.)

## Analog versus Digital

Baseband connections can only transmit digital information (0s and 1s). You cannot use a baseband connection to send sounds across a wire. Broadband, on the other hand, can be either analog (like a telephone line that transmits actual voice frequencies) or digital.

The difference between analog and digital can be described best by comparing an old-type record album with a compact disc (CD). On the record album, sounds were recorded by making physical grooves of various shapes and sizes (i.e. the equivalent of frequency) in the plastic medium. A needle riding on top of those grooves reproduced the sound recorded exactly (along with a few pops and crackles, and perhaps a hiss or two). On a CD, the original sounds were translated into a series of zeros and ones, and then the zeros and ones were stored on the CD by burning the spots with a laser so that they darkened (as opposed to leaving them alone so that they were clear). When the CD was placed in a CD player, another laser read the spots and played the sounds identified by the zeros and ones. There were no pops, crackles, or hisses so the sound was closer to the original. Of course, there are audiophiles who will complain that the sound is not *exactly* the same as the original and that analog reproduces the true sound.

Regardless of the wishes of audiophiles, the world is moving swiftly from analog to digital. Television, for example, will soon be all digital. There are several reasons. Top on the list is the need for more bandwidth, because if you use broadband digitally you can send millions of packets on the same line that previously sent only a single analog transmission (i.e. more channels). But other reasons have influenced the decision; the advent of high density television, as well as the prevalence of video on demand, digital recording devices and other digitally-enabled services. Vendors seeing the potential in these new technologies have pressured the Federal Communications Commission (FCC) into passing a regulation that forces all television stations to transmit only in digital after February 17, 2009 at midnight.

Previously the entertainment networks were analog and the data networks were digital. Now, however, the entertainment network (television and radio) is converging with the digital network (information). This will increase the importance of understanding the underlying IT concepts in how the physical networks work. We will start with the local area networking protocol[33], Ethernet.

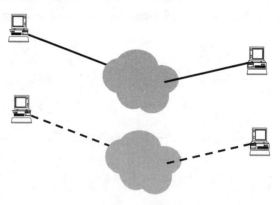

## Ethernet

The most popular choice for LAN protocols is Ethernet. In the eighties there were many others (Token Ring, ArcNet, FDDI, LocalTalk, etc.), but Ethernet has proven to be the most inexpensive with reasonable reliability, so it has become the world-wide standard for LANs. The official name for Ethernet is 802.3, which was established by the Institute for Electrical and Electronic Engineers (IEEE) in January of 1980. Ethernet 802.3 was similar, but not exactly the same, as the Ethernet II, which was the LAN protocol developed by Bob Metcalfe and

**Figure 25  Point to Point circuit versus Packet-based switched network**

---

[33] Remember that *protocol* is just an agreed upon way of doing things. Ethernet is a protocol at the physical networking layer. TCP/IP is the protocol at the logical internetworking layer.

David Boggs a few years before. Both, however, were based upon the same concept: *Packet switching* using *Carrier Sense Multiple Access with Collision Detection* (CSMA/CD).

Packet switching was a different approach to sharing communication medium. Until Ethernet, when one computer wanted to communicate with another computer, they had to establish a circuit - a semi-permanent connection that allowed the two computers to transmit messages back and forth. It didn't matter what medium (fiber, copper wire, satellite, microwave, etc.) actually connected the two computers, the connection was a "circuit" that started up and stayed connected until the computers no longer needed to transmit to each other. The model was based upon the type of connection that was used by the phone company for a telephone call. When two people are talking to each other on analog lines, the connection between them is established upon the first ring and stays on until the last person hangs up.

With packet switching, however, there was no permanent connection of any sort between the two computers (See Figure 25). Instead, each transmission is broken up into millions of datagrams, and each datagram is encapsulated inside a data packet. As illustrated in Figure 26, the implementation of protocols is embedded (or *encapsulated*) within the packet.

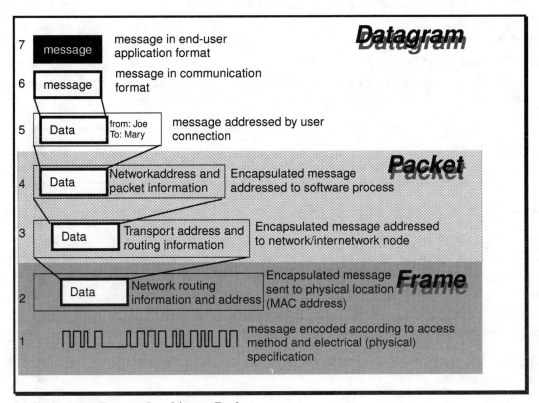

**Figure 26  Datagrams Encapsulated into a Packet**

To send the packet of information, a computer is connected to an Ethernet network interface card (NIC, usually inside the main box) which is then connected to a communication medium (usually an unshielded twisted pair (UTP wire, but can also be a coaxial cable or even a wireless connection). The NIC "listens" to the wire to see if any other device (multiple access) is transmitting (carrier sense). If so, the Ethernet card checks the TO address of the packet and, if appropriate, reads the message and sends it to the waiting application in memory. Otherwise, the NIC waits until the line is clear of all transmissions. When the line is clear, if the NIC has a message to send, it begins transmitting, checking to make sure that no other device is transmitting. If another device transmits at the exact same time (collision detection), the NIC senses the other device and stops transmitting, waiting again until the line is clear of all transmissions.

Keep in mind that this is happening at nano-speeds. A hundred computers can share the line without any problems as long as none of them tries to "hog" the line and transmit continuously (which would prevent all the other computers from being able to transmit at all). Also keep in mind that the information being transmitted is seen by all the computers on the network. It is only protocol that prevents the NIC card from reading the datagram within the packet if it was meant for another NIC card. How does the NIC card know if the message was meant for it? Each NIC card has a unique identifying number known as a Media Access Control (MAC) address that was burned into it when it was manufactured at the factory. The source and destination MAC addresses are found in the outer layers of the every packet (the section known as the data frame) placed there by the sending NIC.

## Frame format

The Ethernet frame's makeup is illustrated in Figure 27. The length of the encapsulated data (application/presentation data, along with session, transport, and network protocol data) can range from 64 to 1500 bytes long, and must be a multiple of 8.

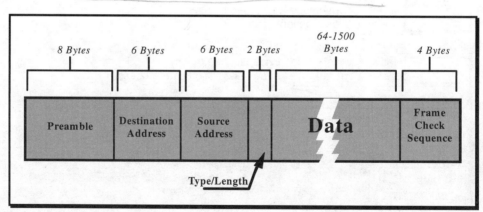

**Figure 27 Ethernet frame**

The different sections of the Ethernet frame are described Table 11.

**Table 11  Ethernet frame breakdown**

| Section | Purpose | Notes |
| --- | --- | --- |
| Preamble / Starting Delimiter | Sets start of frame and synchronizes timing | The preamble is "removed" at the physical layer. |
| Destination address | MAC address of the node the frame is sent to | MAC address is burned into the NIC card by the manufacturer |
| Source address | MAC address of the node generating the frame | Also comes from the NIC card. |
| Length | Length of data field | how many bytes of data |
| Data | Data, including encapsulated higher-level protocols | Varies in length.  Must be a multiple of 8, padded if required. IP address source and destination will be found within the Data |
| Frame Check Sequence | Error checking | Uses Cyclic Redundancy Check (*CRC*) |

The CSMA/CD method of Ethernet seemed like chaos compared to the command-and-control method of Token Ring or ArcNet,  but the ending results proved to be superior and cost effective.  Ethernet transmitted more information at higher speeds with more reliability than the more structured protocols.  As long as the wire didn't get too long  between computers (a transmission can only travel about 100 feet) and as long as none of the computers tried to transmit too often, all the computers on the Ethernet segment could converse easily.

## *Fast Ethernet or GigaEthernet*

The Ethernet protocol has been around for almost two decades and has undergone many changes although all Ethernets start with the same basic CSMA/CD premise.  Originally Ethernet was designed to transmit information at 10 megabits per second (10mbits/s), but newer versions transmit at 100 mbits/s (Fast Ethernet) or 1000 mbits/s (GigaEthernet). Although initially Fast Ethernet and GigaEthernet were only used on backbone segments (the segments that connected all the users together), it is much more common these days to see Fast Ethernet to the desktop and GigaEthernet to servers and powerful users as well as on the backbone.

## *Multiple LANs*

In addition to a limited amount of space between the computers, the number of nodes which can be connected on a single LAN are limited.  Management and performance considerations limit the number of nodes on most Ethernet networks to about eighty, though networks can be connected using switches or routers in order to increase the number of nodes.

A switch is a networking device that has largely replaced bridges and hubs. A bridge was a networking device that connected two networks of dissparate types (such as connecting a Token ring Network to an Ethernet network). Because most networks these days are all of the same type, Ethernet, there is no reason for a bridge.

Every Ethernet network needs a hub. In previous decades there were two kinds of hubs; passive and active. A passive hub didn't do anything except to connect the devices together. An active hub *repeated* the signal so that it could go longer distances. Neither, however, decreased *contention* on the network.

Remember that Ethernet is a CSMA/CD technology. If too many devices on the network are trying to transmit all at the same time, the consequence is a traffic jam that can result in gridlock; no network traffic can get through. Contention is the word applied when there is too much traffic on the network. A switch is a networking device that not only acts as an active hub, but also relieves contention by setting up separate subnets for the Ethernet devices. Instead of 80 computers sharing the same single wire, the switch can be set up to separate out 20 computers on four different wires, thereby decreasing contention and speeding up transmissions. Each individual LAN is considered an Ethernet segment, and the switch can transfer messages between the different segments (without imposing on all the computers on each segment to listen to all the messages on the other segments).

The typical enterprise network, therefore, is actually a collection of many individual LANs. The switches and/or hubs can usually be found within *concentrators* (a frame used to hold a hub or switch) inside the wiring closets that connect to each floor or building.

Now that we've more fully discussed LANs, let's turn to their long distance counterparts, WANs.

# Wide Area Connection (WAN)

If the enterprise network is geographically distributed, it will use long-distance (or "wide area") communications links (such as leased telecommunications lines, leased or company owned fiber optic cabling, microwave links, or even public "switched" networks). These wide area connections make up the Wide Area Network (WAN). An illustration of a WAN can be seen in Figure 28.

*Different Switches*

The term *switch* is another one of those technical terms that has multiple meanings depending upon the context. One type of switch discussed here is the alternative to the hub, a way of connecting Ethernet networking devices to decrease contention and increase length. Long before there was such a thing as Ethernet, however, the telephone company used switches to connect telephone circuits. While the Ethernet switch might be several thousand dollars, the telephone company switch would be several hundred thousand dollars. While the Ethernet switch works with a packet-switched network, the telephone company switch connects analog and leased lines.

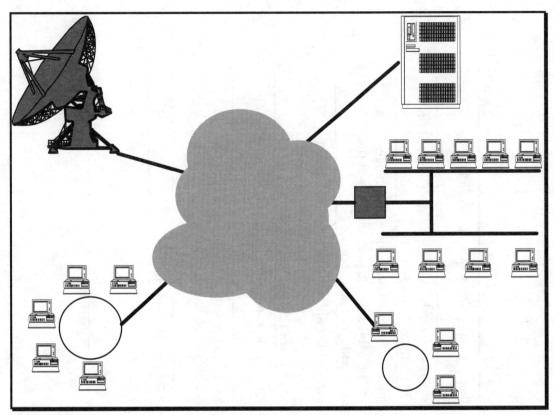

**Figure 28 The WAN: An Enterprise Network**

The internal portion of a WAN system is conceptually represented in Figure 28 as a cloud, a standard method which indicates its operationally-independent nature (i.e. it is usually owned and controlled by the telecommunications company or long distance carrier like Verizon or Sprint/AT&T).

Table 12 summarizes some of the more widely implemented long distance links. The majority of these require special hardware, often supplied, leased, or bought from the long distance carrier or the internet provider supplying the service. Confusion concerning long distance data communications ("long-haul datalinks") can be prevented by keeping track of which acronyms and names are *services* (some of the acronyms are actually service marks), which are standards (and, of course, what the standards refer to), and which simply indicate some technical or physical component of the system. This, of course, is made ever-more difficult by the various technologies and methodologies available, and the vagueness of the practical information available in the market. For instance, T1 is a service named for a technology. "T1" designated the original fully digital telecommunications **T**runk equipment implemented by AT&T, but it has come to mean any point to point leased line.

**Table 12 Types of Long Distance Links (WAN)**

| Type | Service | Notes | Type[34] |
|---|---|---|---|
| RS232C, Vbis, etc. | Modem dial in connections | Standard hardware, ranging from 28 kbit/s to 56 kbit/s | T |
| DSL (Digital Subscriber Line) | Broadband service | A DSL switch (based upon the ADSL protocols). Speed ranges from 128 kbit/s to 3 Mbit/s | S/T |
| Cable Modem | Broadband service | A Cable Modem uses Ethernet protocol. Speed ranges from 384 kbit/s to 8 Mbit/s (but is generally slower due to sharing the line with your neighbors). | S/T |
| FiOS (Fiber Optic Service) | High speed (faster than broadband) service | A new service available only in a few areas that uses a fiber connection to the home or business. Fastest consumer-based service from 2 Mbit/s to 30 Mbit/s. | S/T |
| T1 (also known as Leased Lines) | Point to Point connection at T1 connection speeds. | 1.544 Mbit/s transmission speed. Requires PBX and/or special hardware. | S/T |
| Fractional T1 | Same as T1, but partial bandwidth service, not a full 1.544 Mbit/s. | Blocks of 64 Kbit/s bandwidth. Multiple blocks can be multiplexed, possibly on demand. | S |
| T3 | Multiplexed T1 lines | 28 T1 lines, 44.7 Mbit/s bandwidth. | S |
| Fractional T3 | An alternate method of marketing multiple T1 lines | Same as T1 and T3. | S |

---

[34] S denotes a Service, T denotes a specific technology. If the type can be considered either a service or a technology, S/T is used.

| Type | Service | Notes | Type[34] |
|---|---|---|---|
| Frame Relay | High-speed access method, point to point but allows virtual connection speeds that change dynamically. | Relays the LAN frame with minimal in-band overhead (virtual circuits) | S |
| ISDN (Integrated Services Digital Network) | High-speed link, various services | ISDN was touted for many years as a faster alternative to dialup lines, but have been pushed out of the market by DSL and cable modem. Still available and used for special purposes like dedicated video conferencing links.  Speed is 128 kbit/s. | S/T |
| ATM[35] (Asynchronous Transfer Mode) | Intermediate long-haul access method for specialized services | Used by ISPs and telecommunication service companies.  Speeds range from 155 Mbit/s to 622 Mbit/s. | S/T |
| SONET (Synchronous Optical Network) (Also known as Optical Carrier (as in OC-1, OC-3, OC-12, and OC-255). | Service offered by AT&T, refers long-haul fiber access method | Flexible, fiber optic backbone long-haul services, from 52 Mbit/s to 13 Gbit/s. | S/T |

[35] Do not confuse the ATM access method with an Automatic Teller Machine (also called an ATM).  They are not in any way related.

# Physical Cabling

Most wiring systems were originally installed to carry voice telephone transmissions. Most telephone wiring systems use *structured wiring* for the general layout (centralized "wiring closets" to wall plates in each office). When data wiring began being installed in office buildings, it only made sense to use structured wiring as well. However, there is one major difference: in voice systems: for the most part, the quality of wire used is quite low compared to that required for data cabling.

The signals that are sent over telephone wires are extremely low frequency (approx. 5 to 15000 Kilohertz), and analog in nature. The wire installed to carry the signals is not up to the task of sending 10 or 100 Megahertz digital signals, particularly so because high-speed electronic equipment is far less forgiving of minor signal fluctuations than the human ear.

## *Common transmission problems*

All LAN systems which deal with the physical layers of the network must address some fundamental difficulties inherent in electromagnetic transmissions. The problems involved in transmitting data bit streams across a physical cable are universal, regardless of whether the information is transmitted through "open air" broadband transmissions, or across point-to-point cabling systems using baseband techniques, although the particular affects on transmission will vary, obviously, between the two systems.

The primary difficulties that are encountered on all LAN systems include attenuation, cross-talk, jitter, and signal interference.

**Attenuation** is a loss of signal strength due to distance. Attenuation can be a result of poor signal strength, impedance[36] mismatch, poor quality conductors, or other problems with the physical configuration of the network.

**Crosstalk** is a result of electromagnetic radiation of the signal outside of the wire carrying the transmission. In some respects, all wires can act as antennae, both transmitting signals to and receiving signals from other cables in physical proximity. This is especially true in the case of cables which run side-by-side for some distance.

**Near-End-Crosstalk** (often abbreviated as NEXT) is a transmission difficulty associated with systems which use separate conductors for transmission and reception. When the signal is sent (at "full strength") on the transmission line, an incoming signal on the receiver line (which has been attenuated during its propagation on the wire) can "get clobbered", or be drowned out, by the more powerful, out-going signal.

One of the techniques for controlling cross-talk, of course, is the use of shielded cables. Additionally, twisting the conductors of paired-conductor cabling also decreases crosstalk. (Electrically, twisting the conductors around each other is very similar to using a separate

---

[36] Impedance is measured in Ohms and refers to the relationship between the current and the voltage of a cable. the An excellent non-technical explanation of impedance can be found at http://forum.ecoustics.com/bbs/messages/34579/131527.html, written on April 12, 2005 and sponsored by ecoustics.com, a Hi-fi on-line retailer. Accessed May, 2008.

shield element.) Higher quality cable (better shielding, tighter twists, etc.) and connectors decrease near-end crosstalk, while precision circuitry can decrease its effects.

A cumulative destabilizing effect on the timing of signals, **jitter** is the result of minor inaccuracies in the transmission of a signal, frequency attenuation (the tendency of signal-carrying systems to attenuate some frequencies more than others), and signal clocking (inaccurate timing of the carrier signal).

EMI (Electro-Magnetic Interference) is caused by something from an outside system. Simply switching on the lights in an office, for instance, usually creates enough of a radiated electromagnetic "spike" of transmitted electrical energy that it can interrupt network transmissions and cause either crosstalk or jitter. Note that fiber optic cabling, because it does not use electrical signals, is immune to electromagnetic interference.)

## Frame distribution

Structured wiring (the method of wiring used by AT&T) was used in most buildings for both voice and data cabling. This required the use of *distribution frames* The basic concept of frame distribution is centralized, point-to-point wiring. A Main Distribution Frame (MDF, see Figure 29) refers to cabling between floors, buildings, or areas. Within the MDF, Intermediate Distribution Frames (IDF) are used to distribute the signal service to individual locations.

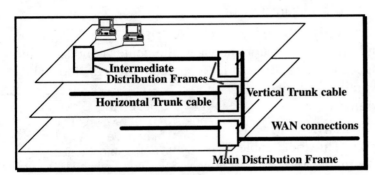

**Figure 29 Distribution frames**

On a practical level, the use of distribution frames simply indicates centralized wiring closets in each area, with direct cabling to each office from the wiring closet.

## Star Topology

As mentioned earlier, the star topology is the preferred and predominant physical wiring scheme, though the electrical topology of most networks varies. (The mesh topology, discussed in the Internetworking chapter, referred to a *logical* topology. When we are talking about Ethernet, we are discussing a *physical* topology. The logical topology of Ethernet is a bus topology, but the physical topology is a star.)

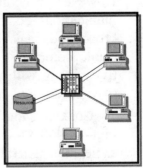

In the star topology, as shown in Figure 30, all nodes are connected to a single point. While requiring longer cable lengths than any other

**Figure 30 Star topology (physical)**

standard topology, this geometry enables the easiest management, maintenance, and reconfigurations.

## Types of Network Cables

The cable used by the trunk and the user connections (nodes) can be of two different types. Trunk cable is generally designed for heavy duty use, while the node connections use lighter cabling to wire individual offices.

In a standard wiring plant *patch cables* link the individual ports in the concentrator to a *patch panel*, or *punch-down block*.

The patch panel (simply an array of connectors) or punch-down block is connected, in turn, to the installed wiring running through the floors, ceilings, wiring ducts, walls, and/or elevator shafts and risers of the building. This cabling connects at the wall plate in the offices. Additional patch cables connect the wall connector to the user's equipment (NIC).

There are three different types of cable used in most networks; coaxial, unshielded twisted pair, and fiber optic.

### Coaxial cable

Coaxial cable consists of a center conductor within an insulation core. Metal braiding is wrapped around the core, and covered by a heavy-duty jacket. Coaxial cable comes in a variety of specification with differing electrical characteristics.

Coaxial cable is primarily characterized by its impedance characteristics. The size of the center conductor and the distance (and type of insulator) between the center conductor and braided "shield" determines the impedance and bandwidth characteristics of the cable. Generally, the thicker the cable overall, the lower the impedance, and the greater the bandwidth.

Coaxial cable is rather expensive, and difficult to work with. Especially with the thicker (1/2") "Thicknet" cable, installation is severely affected. Due to the rise of unshielded twisted pair wiring as well as the cost and lengthy installation time, the amount of coaxial cable being used in modern networks had decreased in the early nineties. However, in addition to being used for digital data communications, coax is heavily used for analog and/or broadband transmissions, such as video and satellite links. Cable companies are beginning to sell network connectivity along with television services, and this has led to a rise in the use of coaxial cable for networks.

> All wire is not equal. Even two lengths of cable which appear identical may have slightly (or widely!) differing electrical performance. Specifically, with UTP (unshielded twisted pair) cabling, the "quality" of the cable varies tremendously. Coaxial cable is far more resistant to the environment (including physical variations in temperature, etc. as well as electrical interference) since it has shielding. However, though electrically superior to UTP, Coax is usually far more expensive.

Coaxial cable typically uses BNC connectors. The BNC connectors can be seen in Figure 34. To preserve the electrical characteristics of the cable system, unconnected coaxial cable ends generally require a terminator.

**Figure 31 BNC Connector for coaxial cable**

### *Unshielded Twisted Pair (UTP)*

Unshielded twisted pair is currently the most popular type of cabling. Any number of pairs (usually 4, but it could be 1 to 25) of wire can be contained within the same cable sheath, with each pair of wires twisted around itself (see Figure 32). While UTP is the easiest to install and the cheapest of the standard cable types used for data networks, the quality of unshielded twisted pair cabling also varies greatly.

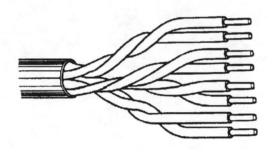

**Figure 32  UTP cabling (4 pair)**

The quality of unshielded twisted pair cabling is determined by the size of the conductor, the thickness and type of insulating jackets, and **most importantly** (from a data network viewpoint) **the number of twists per foot**. Twists per foot affect the electrical characteristics of the wire. In effect, the "tighter" the twists, the less high frequency signal energy can "leak out". That is, the more twists per foot, the greater the bandwidth of the cable. (It should be obvious that, since the twists in the wire pairs are a vital characteristic in the electrical performance of the cable, the two wires used for a connection **must** be a single twisted pair. You cannot use wires from two different pairs to carry data.)

This vital statistic, twists per foot, will vary between cables from different manufacturers, and even varies between the individual pairs in a single cable sheath. Because the outside twisted pairs are usually wrapped around the inner twisted pairs, giving them a larger circumference in proportion to the inner pairs, which are twisted around each other, the inner pairs may have more twists per foot. This varies, of course, based on the manufacturing methods and the number of pairs in the cable.

The quality of the UTP cable is categorized as 1,2,3,4,5 or 6. "Regular" telephone wiring (referred to as DIW, *Direct Indoor Wiring*) is often low-grade unshielded twisted pair and is category 1 or 2. (The majority of the office wiring is generally untwisted, but the trunk cables are twisted to reduce interference and noise.) The Ethernet specification (also called *10BaseT*) specifies UTP category 3 or higher, although most installations today use category 5.

The type of connector used for most end-connections of voice UTP and untwisted pair wiring is **RJ-11.**. It is not often used for data network connections. The connector has 4 contacts, and is relatively narrow. (Figure 0–1) The connector widely used for data network UTP connections is **RJ-45.** RJ-45 connectors are very similar to RJ-11, though slightly wider and it usually has 8 contacts. Both can be seen in Figure 33.

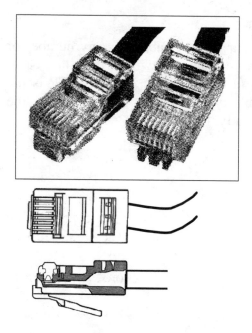

**Figure 33  RJ-11 & RJ-45 UTP connectors**

### *Fiber*

Fiber optic cable is a glass or plastic thread surrounded by a cladding. The cladding is in turn surrounded by a protective plastic coating (see Figure 34).

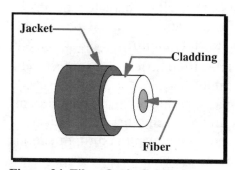

**Figure 34  Fiber Optic Cabling**

Unlike any other cable, fiber optic cable does not carry data via electrical impulses. Instead, the signal is converted to light using a laser or LED (light emitting diode). The light impulses can travel immense distances through the fiber with minimal attenuation. Because the energy is not electrical, the signal is completely immune to noise and electromagnetic interference (including crosstalk and voltage spikes). Since the light impulses are contained within the cladding (as shown in Figure 35.) and do not "radiate" as electrical impulses do, fiber optic transmissions are more secure than electrical transmission methods.

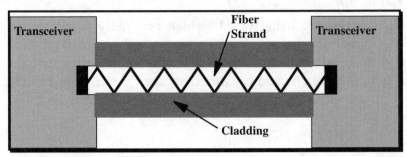

**Figure 35  Fiber optics**

The fiber optic cable used in most data networks utilize the less expensive plastic fiber and LED light sources. The cable is identified by the diameter of the fiber and the cladding.

Fiber optic cable is the most expensive type of standard networking cable, so it is rarely used for internal house or building wiring. The installation of fiber optic cable can also be difficult and costly, since special skills and tools are required, and the connections must be much more precise than with electrical wire.

Most connectors used with fiber optic cable are *ST* (Straight Tip) bayonet-style connectors. Similar to, but smaller than, BNC connectors used with coaxial cable, ST (or just *S*) connectors are "push-on, twist-to-lock" connections. As mentioned previously, these connectors require special skills and tools to install.

# Wireless

Like its wired counterpart, the first use of wireless communication was for voice. Radio and television have broadcasted wirelessly since the beginning. Also mentioned, however, was that analog voice broadcasts use the bandwidth differently than data communications. Even wireless cell phone networks were originally analog.

Eventually, however, wireless communications are becoming digital. As mentioned earlier in the chapter, on February 17, 2009 in the United States there will be no more analog television, only digital.

Wireless does, however, have one large advantage over wired; no need for installed cables. When we discussed the First Mile Crisis in the first chapter, it was noted that in 2002 the first mile crisis was expected to cost 365 billion dollars. In the United States the majority of the crisis is being solved by wired solutions; DSL, Cable Modem, and FiOS. In Europe and other countries, however, wireless became the more frequent choice. As a result, wireless capability has grown drastically within the last ten years - but not as fast in the United States as elsewhere.

Unfortunately, wireless options are not yet as standardized as wired options, and are changing much more frequently. Furthermore, wireless options are complicated by the fact that world governments are starting to regulate the use of wireless networking frequencies along with the radio and television frequencies they have regulated in the past. We will discuss several types of wireless networks; GSM/EDGE, CDMA/EVDO, UMB, WiFi/WiMax, and Bluetooth.

## *Global System for Mobile Communication (GSM)*

Eighty-two percent of cellular phones are using GSM (which originally stood for the European group that developed it, *Groupe Spécial Mobile*). You can tell if your cell phone is GSM because it will have a SIM (Subscriber Identify Module) card imbedded within the phone. If you take the SIM card out of the phone and put it into another phone, your cellular identity (along with your list of phone numbers and voice mail connection) will be transferred to the new phone.

GSM includes Short Message Service (SMS) which allows users to send short text messages to other users. However, GMS uses a time-sharing method of multiplexing (sharing the wire) which is too slow for any other type of data communication. In 1997 General Packet Radio Service (GPRS) was released which enabled devices such as Blackberry to send and receive email messages. However, even that was not really adequate for real connectivity to the Internet or to corporate resources such as servers or databases. Enhanced Data Rates for GMS Evolution (EDGE) was the answer, introduced in 1999. It can transmit data up to 236.8 kbit/s (faster than dialup, but still not close to broadband speeds).

## *Code Division Multiple Access (CDMA)*

Used mostly in the United States, CDMA has slightly higher bandwidth out of the gate than GSM, and requires the use of a specific handset that cannot be used with other networks (because there is no SIM card). It breaks up the signal into packets instead of multiplexing the circuit in time. It is still, however, not good enough for true data connectivity, so CDMA2000 and EVDO (Evolution Data Optimized) are designed using the same methodology as CDMA, but allowing from 1 to 14.7 Mbits/s.

## *Ultra Mobile Broadband (UMB)*

There is plan in the works for a wireless data connection that utilizes the networks of the GSM and more efficient packet transmission of CDMA called Ultra Mobile Broadband. At this time, UMB is still just theoretical, but many expect it to be the next generation of wireless connectivity for both voice and data.

## *Bluetooth*

Bluetooth is not, actually, a wireless networking method in the usual sense. It can only connect devices that are in very close proximity to each other such as a cell phone transmitter and a wireless earphone, or a laptop computer and its printer. (Prior to Bluetooth, for a computer to connect with a printer wirelessly, they both needed infrared transceivers, required line-of-site, and was often unreliable). Bluetooth is often used is what is called *personal area networks (PAN)* as opposed to LANs or WANs. The speed is between 1 and 3 Mbit/s. It was approved as a standard by the IEEE as 802.15.

### *Wi-Fi*

Whereas Ethernet is the protocol for wired LANs (IEEE standard 802.3), Wi-Fi is the protocol for wireless LANs (IEEE standard 802.11). People can purchase a Wi-Fi hub and router combination at their local office supply store and set up a Wi-Fi network relatively easily. Most laptop computers come with a Wi-Fi NIC already installed and set up to automatically sense Wi-Fi networks in the area. Businesses can install a Wi-Fi network and allow their customers to use it, generally known as a Hot Spot. Speeds range from 4 Mbit/s to 120 Mbit/s.

One of the early difficulties with Wi-Fi was its use of power - it is considered a power hog, and therefore is not a good alternative for PANs. Another problem is security, although nowadays most people use WEP (Wired Equivalent Privacy) to encrypt data sent across their Wi-Fi so that others can't read it, and  WPA (Wi-Fi Protected Access) to prevent unauthorized use of the wireless network.

Another problem with Wi-Fi is its relatively small area - it can only reach between 100 and 300 meters. When Wi-Fi networks are connected together, they often use another wireless protocol that was designed to cover large areas, WiMAX (Wireless Interoperability for Microwave Access), also an IEEE standard 802.16 or WirelessMAN for Wireless Metropolitan Area Networks.

## Top Down - the Whole Map

We have not tranversed the entire technology map from top to bottom. Although the information provided in this book is only accurate for the time frame in which is was written, understanding this information will provide an excellent foundation for non-technical people to be able to talk to technical people (and not make a fool of themselves) and make good business decisions regarding technology.

As noted initially, this book is designed as a supplemental book to either *Microsoft Office in Business* or *The Entrepreneur's Guide to Managing Information Technology* (or both for the truly ambitious). If you have any questions or comments, contact the author.

# INDEX

melissa  1 EF  Pfistner
215 - 536 - 0791